Palmistry
Revealed

This book is dedicated to my little Rinpoche,
who reconnected me to life when I thought I'd lost the thread.
In my darkest hour, I was given perfection,
I hope I will always remain grateful.

Palmistry Revealed

A simple guide
to unlocking the secrets
of your hands

Paul Fenton-Smith

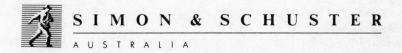

SIMON & SCHUSTER
AUSTRALIA

With special thanks to Cathy, a Venusian who offered to help and tactfully edited my many drafts without treading on my Girdle of Venus; to Amanda for being patient; to Pauline for encouraging me to write; and to Alexander for all the joy. Thanks also to those who allowed me to photograph their hands, and to Margaret Hastie for the illustrations.

PALMISTRY REVEALED

First published in Australasia in 1996 by
Simon & Schuster Australia
20 Barcoo Street, East Roseville NSW 2069

Viacom International
Sydney New York London Toronto Tokyo Singapore

National Library of Australia
Cataloguing-in-Publication data

Fenton-Smith, Paul.
    Palmistry revealed : a simple guide to unlocking the
    secrets of your hands.

    Bibliography.
    Includes index.
    ISBN 0 7318 0588 7.

    1. Palmistry. 2. Palmistry — Handbooks, manuals, etc.
    I. Title.

133.6

Cover designed by Anna Warren
Cover photograph by Craig Cranko
Designed by Joy Eckermann
Illustrations by Margaret Hastie
Printed in Australia by McPherson's
The 'Palmistry Hand' illustrated on the cover is manufactured by Dynamo House,
4–10 Yorkshire Street, Richmond, Vic. 3121. Tel. (03) 94283636.

Contents

Introduction

WHY READ THE HANDS?

Palmistry is a science, and by carefully examining the size, shape, colour, texture, flexibility, moisture, lines, signs and markings on both sides of both hands we can learn a great deal about a person. No two hands are the same — the left and right hands will have subtle (and sometimes obvious) differences.

Our hands are a window to our souls. They reflect our nature, our qualities and detail those events in our past which have shaped our beliefs about life. We all have a need to be loved, to be listened to and to be happy, yet each of us has a different approach to fulfilling these needs.

Some people sit awhile and, in their stillness, draw to themselves those things they desire. Others leap up and go in search of their goals, believing that nothing happens unless they make it happen. Both approaches work. The first if you are patient, the second if you have the energy.

A close study of your hands will confirm your preferred approach and the sort of things which fulfil you. By reading your hands carefully, you will discover your strengths and weaknesses. The study of palmistry offers us a glimpse into the lives of ourselves and others and, in turn, a glimpse of life itself.

A friend and I once spent a weekend with my friend's great-uncle at his holiday cottage. Uncle Walter, as we called him, asked me how I earned a living, and I told him I was a palmist. The logs hissed wildly as the fire engulfed them, and he placed his trembling hands, palms downwards, on the makeshift table between us. Long, knotty fingers and ridged, fluted nails with very small moons were the first things I noticed. The small moons in his nails explained the open fire roaring away on what was a warm autumn afternoon. They indicated that his blood circulation was poor, leaving his hands and feet quite cold. I gently touched his hands and confirmed my judgement. Still, at the age of 88 he had the right to slow down a little. I, too, will probably need a fire in my old age.

We talked long into the evening, adding logs to the fire and topping up the teapot. Most of what I told him was history, and his vivid memory confirmed much of what I gleaned from his hands.

His hands held only one Relationship Line. It was forked, with one branch moving down to cross the Line of Heart (a sign of divorce or death of the partner or the relationship) and the other branch continuing steadily into the Mount of Mercury. I explained that I was puzzled, as it seemed that he had lost his partner but that the relationship had continued. He smiled and nodded. 'Yes, that's right. She died when I was 67, yet I still love her. When it's my time to go I'll be happy to go, for I'll be rejoining her.'

I recently read for a man in his early fifties and told him that he would have made a good doctor; in particular, a surgeon. As a second career choice, I suggested psychology. I also told him that he would have to be careful not to give up his ambitions for someone he loved, for such a sacrifice could prove worthless.

He later explained that he had given up medical studies in his twenties to follow a young woman overseas, and that she had married someone else. He then completed a psychology degree, and had recently closed his private practice to follow another woman to Australia.

Most major events are visible in our hands long before they actually occur, and forewarned is forearmed. If you know something is going to happen *before* it happens, you can prepare for it or change your course.

At birth we are each given a map, stamped into our skin so we don't lose it. It is astounding to observe the clear lines, signs and markings on the hands of children only hours or days old, and to realise that there is a destiny to match the map they carry. These maps detail people they will meet, who they will marry and even the children they will have. This map on our hands means that, most times, a solution to a problem is within our grasp. The use of free will determines whether we follow this map or change it.

I remember reading the hands of a nine-year-old girl and I mentioned the three children she will probably give birth to in the future. The girl's eyes widened, and I could see that she had never thought she would be a mother herself one day. Even her grandchildren showed on her hand. It felt strange to give predictions of events which could occur long after I have passed away.

Care is called for when reading hands, as hasty judgements made after a quick glance at someone's hands can lead to errors. There are often contradictory signs to be found in the hands. The person might be arrogant yet sensitive, forgetful yet very good at remembering numbers, or quick-minded yet dreamy. It is important to examine the hands carefully before saying anything.

This book is laid out in the order in which I would give a palm reading. This method results in the least number of contradictions when reading hands. There are bound to be contradictions in your hands, for who you appear to be and who you are deep within can be quite different.

WHY DOES PALMISTRY WORK?

The hands and the brain are closely connected by nerves. The brain instructs the hands to perform intricate tasks, such as writing, grasping objects or playing musical instruments. In turn, the hands relay to the brain important information such as temperature, texture and so on.

This two-way communication is constant in our waking state and is often automatic, or subconscious. Once we have learned to eat with a knife and fork, for instance, we no longer need to think consciously about how we are going to cut up a piece of food and place it into our mouths. We do it automatically, often as we talk, listen or think about something else. Our hands, however, are still busy informing our brains that we hold a knife and fork, and our brains are still transmitting to our hands what to do with them so that we can eat.

This complicated flow of nerve impulses between the brain and the hands is not without its side effects. This exchange of energy gradually changes the lines and mounts (the fleshy pads on the palm) on the hands. 'As a man thinks, so he becomes' is an old saying that truly captures what palmistry is about. By examining someone's hands, we can learn something about the person and his or her approach to life.

As incidents and decisions shape our lives, corresponding lines appear on our hands. The shape of our hands and the lines on our palms tell of forthcoming events and of our most likely decisions when these situations are upon us. Most of our reactions to future problems and challenges will be based on past experiences and decisions. It follows that through a careful examination of our past and our present circumstances, we can determine our responses to future events.

Although our hands foretell the future, that future is not fixed. It holds many different possibilities from which we are free to select. By exercising our free will and making decisions, we are able to change the course of our lives from that moment forward, despite what is foretold in our hands.

Part I
The basics

FINGERS

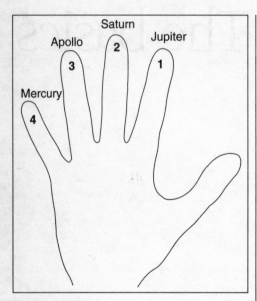

Saturn
Apollo 2 Jupiter
3 1
Mercury
4

Figure 1 *The fingers*

Opportunities for observing fingers and thumbs abound for the budding palmist: from the person reading a newspaper on the train to the man or woman giving you change at the local sandwich shop.

When reading someone's hands, it makes sense to examine the fingers and thumbs first, for you can do this long before someone opens his or hands to you for a reading. My palm readings often begin at the front door as I welcome my client. We shake hands, and I notice the hand temperature, moisture and the shape of the fingernails. The fingers also represent the outer personality, so it is logical to start with

the outer self then work inwards. The fingers on the hand are numbered from one to four and each is named after a planet. (In this book, they are referred to by their planetary name.) Each finger represents a certain aspect of personality, as follows:

- **First finger (index) — Jupiter**
The first finger represents ambition, independent ideas and beliefs, religious or philosophic needs, and inner confidence.

- **Second finger (middle) — Saturn**
The second finger represents balance (between introversion and extroversion, work and play, responsibility and freedom), responsibility, reputation and long-term plans.

- **Third finger (ring) — Apollo**
The third finger represents creative abilities, self-expression (e.g. acting, writing, talking, athletics, dance), gambling tendencies and a love of beautiful objects and surroundings.

- **Fourth finger (little) — Mercury**
The fourth finger represents communication, business ability, the ability to remember numbers, mathematics, medicine, mimicry and quick thought.

Gaps between the fingers

A noticeable gap between the Jupiter and Saturn fingers indicates a healthy confi-

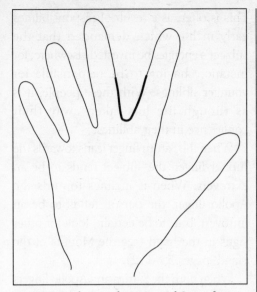

Figure 2 *Gap between the Jupiter and Saturn fingers*

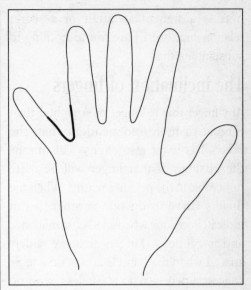

Figure 4 *Gap between the Apollo and Mercury fingers*

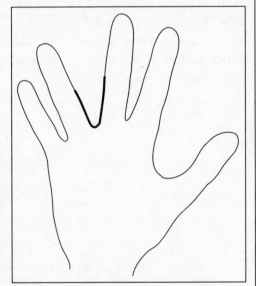

Figure 3 *Gap between the Saturn and Apollo fingers*

dence and self-worth. These people often have a religious or spiritual philosophy that is independent of those around them.

An unusually wide gap between the Saturn and Apollo fingers indicates some-

one with little or no concern for what tomorrow holds. This is a rare thing to see in the hands, and I recall two examples in particular: an elderly lady who was dying of cancer and lived only for the day, and a young girl who had recently recovered from what was believed to be a terminal illness. This girl made no plans for tomorrow and lived only for the moment.

People with a gap between the Apollo and Mercury fingers strive to keep themselves separate from what they are communicating. For instance, a salesperson with this gap may be able to communicate clearly and easily when it comes to a product or concept, but will find it difficult to express feelings and emotions.

I have observed that people with a wide gap between the Apollo and Mercury fingers can be hard to get close to on an emotional level. Some palmists believe that a wide gap here is a sign of an affair or a secret relationship, but I have found nothing to substantiate this.

The inclination of fingers

Any finger that is longer or straighter than normal or more independent than the others has fewer restrictions. This means the qualities of that finger will be more noticeable in the person's nature. When the fingers curve in on one another, it can indicate someone who lacks self-confidence and is cautious. Fingers that are widely spaced when the hand is at rest on a table suggest a person who is careless, with no thought for tomorrow. This carelessness can extend to money, secrets and material possessions.

When the Jupiter finger inclines towards the Saturn finger, it suggests a lack of confidence to pursue goals and ambitions.

This is often as a result of responsibilities early in life which demanded that the subject's energies be invested elsewhere; for instance, having to be responsible for younger siblings. With these people, it is as though life has taken away their confidence in their abilities.

When the Saturn finger leans towards the Jupiter finger, the subject tends to be an extrovert. When it inclines towards the Apollo finger, the person tends to be an introvert, but, to be certain, look for other signs in the hand (see the Mounts of the Hand, pages 55–112).

When both the Saturn and Apollo fingers incline towards one another, the subject often has a great sense of responsibility and duty. These people find it difficult to take a break and rest during a project, for their minds will usually be focused on the work that is yet to be completed.

THE THUMBS

Thumbs are an important part of hand reading, for while the fingers describe personality and the palms detail events throughout life, the thumbs describe our inner nature, willpower and logic or reasoning ability. For instance, someone with conic fingers and a square thumb would be attracted to change or novelty; impulsive on the surface yet steady and somewhat conservative underneath due to the square thumb. This person would mix well with conic-handed people, yet be more at home with square-handed types (see Part II).

In some parts of India and Asia, palmistry consists of reading the thumbs only. The thumb is a central part of the analysis for that particular system of hand reading.

Thumb position

The thumb can be set high, medium or low on the hand, and the lower the thumb, the higher the person's intelligence and the greater his or her adaptability to circumstance.

A low-set thumb will reach to the base of the Jupiter finger. This type of thumb shows ability to adapt easily to any circumstance and the ability to achieve goals.

An average length medium-set thumb will reach to the middle of the third phalange of the Jupiter finger, when held straight alongside the palm. This type of thumb shows a balance between adaptability to circumstance and an ability to change circumstances when the need arises.

A high-set thumb will reach almost to the middle of the Jupiter finger. This type of thumb signifies a decreased ability to adapt to circumstance, often resulting in a deeper sense of frustration.

During a battle or a competitive situation, people will sometimes fold their thumbs inside their closed palms or clenched fists. This indicates that they surrender their will to the situation or the other person.

An example of this occurred when I was driving past the scene of a car accident one day. As the drivers engaged in a lengthy argument over who was to blame for the accident, I noticed the younger man fold his thumbs inside his closed palms. It indicated to me that he had mentally surrendered to the other person. I watched closely for a few minutes, long enough to see him put forward his final argument and then accept the blame.

It is significant how close the thumb sits to the hand when the hands are resting on the table. Place both hands palm downwards on the table. Then turn both hands over and notice whether the thumb curls

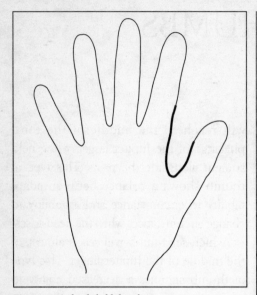

Figure 5 *A closely held thumb*

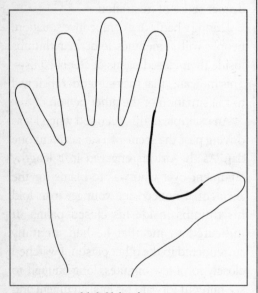

Figure 6 *A widely held thumb*

in on the hand. If it does, the person is less likely to assert his or her will. If the non-writing hand's thumb curls inwards, it shows someone who tends to surrender his or her will as an adult.

The more space there is between the thumb and the hand, the more independent the subject is. A hand with a thumb at a wide angle (60 degrees or more) indicates someone who is generous, independent, sympathetic, enjoys freedom and extends freedom of thought and action to others.

The closer the thumb is to the hand when relaxed, the closer the person keeps his or her motives and thoughts. When the thumb lies quite close to the hand, it indicates someone who tends to be secretive, cautious and less sympathetic to the joys and sorrows of others.

The medium-set thumb, which is not too close to the hand and not too far away from it, indicates a well-balanced person. Reasonable and tolerant, these people are ruled by their hearts *and* their minds.

The phalanges

Note the length of each phalange of the thumb. The first (or nail) phalange is usually a little shorter than the second, while the third is almost half the entire length of the thumb, from its tip to the chain of lines across the base of the hand at the wrist (the rascette).

Note the firmness and fullness of each phalange. Willpower, decisiveness and the ability to command others are qualities of the first phalange. One or two vertical lines on the first phalange can indicate that others are willing to assist the subject in fulfilling his or her will. One or two horizontal lines can describe opposition from others.

The second (or middle) phalange represents perception, reasoning ability, judgement and logical analysis. A single vertical line on this phalange can indicate assistance in reasoning or logical analysis; for instance, as a child, the subject may have been encouraged to reason or debate aloud those issues which were important to him or her and, in turn, this may have encouraged a reliance on reasoning ability.

A single horizontal line on the second phalange can describe obstacles to the subject's reasoning abilities; impatience for action or a passionate nature, for instance, can make it difficult for someone's reasoning mind to sort through the alternatives.

A friend of mine has a thick horizontal line across this second phalange and he laughingly tells a story about his childhood that is a typical example of the cause of this type of line. When he was eight years old, his father sat him down and told him that he must continue to study hard and attend university after completing school because 'after you leave school, your brain goes to sleep'. He said that he sat there in shock, wondering what he had done to deserve a complete fool for a father. There was no encouragement for my friend to polish his logic or reasoning skills as a child.

The third phalange (including the Mount of Venus — see pages 104–107) details the capacity for love, sympathy and passion.

The combination of these three phalanges describes our moral force — the proportion of willpower, reasoning ability, tact in dealing with others and stubbornness or flexibility of mind.

Thumb size

Note the overall size of the thumb in relation to the hand. Large thumbs show force of character, small thumbs a lack of force. The shorter the thumb, the more easygoing the person tends to be.

Large-thumbed people are those who naturally rule, as their will and reasoning abilities are well developed. They usually prefer useful, necessary and practical things, and generally display more determination than those with shorter thumbs. Small thumbs belong to those with a romantic and sentimental outlook. These people enjoy beauty and creativity.

Thumb shape

People with a bulging first phalange can display stubbornness and determination, and are likely to fly into a rage when opposed. Their will can override their logic, and they may fail to learn from mistakes. Others may consider them to be obstinate, as they stick to their guns even when shown a better way of doing something.

Louise showed me Martin's hands soon after they started seeing each other. The first thing I noticed was the bulging first phalanges of his thumbs. I made a mental note to observe the effect of these thumbs in action. Over the course of their two-year relationship, I saw Louise give up a great deal of herself and her interests in favour of Martin's interests. When they separated, Martin divided all their possessions, selecting for himself all the things he wanted, and then drove away. Martin didn't even need to fight for those things he wanted, for Louise had been sufficiently worn down by his stubborn determination and offered no resistance.

A clubbed thumb (a thumb with a club-like first phalange) depicts someone who has very strong will. It was traditionally called 'the murderer's thumb', however I have found that people with a clubbed thumb can usually count on one hand the number of times they have lost their temper in their life.

When angry, these people will usually become very pale and begin to shake. At this point they often walk away from the person or the situation causing the tension. They seem to know instinctively that if they were to stay in the situation, they might do something they would later regret. This is due to their tendency to suppress their feelings until they want to explode, at which point they know they are likely to act without reason.

While people with this type of thumb are not necessarily murderers, on occasion they will require great self-discipline to overcome their temper. Often they do not express anger over smaller incidents, allowing tension to build up to an un-bearable level.

A longer second phalange than first indicates someone with excess energy in their logic and reasoning, giving them great reasoning ability but little will to act upon their plans. These types can clearly see how to improve a system or situation, but may do very little to act upon what they believe.

They sometimes prefer talk to action.

If the thumb is wide and has first and second phalanges of equal width, it can indicate someone who gives little thought to how their actions affect others. They can appear ignorant and unreasonable, doing as they please, to the point of walking over others. They care little for refinement in dress, word, actions or eating. This disregard for the opinions of others can assist them to be more successful in business as they have the ability to push their way to the top, asserting themselves forcefully when they feel that force is required.

Some years back I spent a frustrating three weeks working for a man with this type of thumb. He would never allow me to complete a sale in his small accessories shop without interrupting my conversation with the customer and taking over. He was in a constant state of terror that one of his employees might lose a sale. He would phone me late at night and bark a question down the line without so much as an introduction. 'Where did you put the stock report, Paul?' or 'How many sales did you make today?' I grew tired of this very quickly and soon took to answering the phone at night with a heavy foreign accent, ex-plaining that Paul was asleep or out for the evening.

When the thumb is not very wide and yet the first and second phalanges are the same width, it describes a person with strong determination and good physical strength. These people can be more aware of others, more refined, yet can still sometimes remain somewhat forthright or even aggressive.

When the second phalange is narrower than the first, and has a waist-like appearance, the subject is likely to display great tact and diplomacy. These people rarely rub others the wrong way and achieve their plans with little opposition. Others often enjoy helping them to succeed because of their tactful approach.

The musician's thumb

A thumb which appears to be made up of three separate and distinctly angled sections is known as a musician's thumb. People with this type of thumb have a well-developed sense of rhythm and are more likely be drawn to rhythm instruments (drums, bass, etc.) or music with a notice-

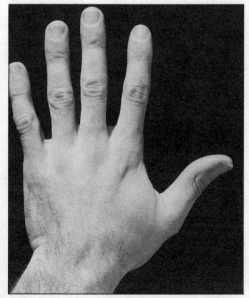

Figure 7 *The musician's thumb*

able rhythm than to melody or harmony instruments (piano, saxophone, etc.).

Years ago, when I played in a band, we were auditioning drummers. One young man proved to be completely lacking in any sense of rhythm and timing and I felt compelled to examine his hands. He did not possess a musician's thumb. I asked him why he chose the drums and he confided that he really wanted to be a singer, but that his last band had pointed out that he lacked a sense of pitch so he became a drummer by default.

The drummer we eventually chose had very noticeable angles on his thumbs, and he tightened the whole sound of the band by giving us all a strong and clear rhythm and a sense of purpose.

The musician's thumb doesn't necessarily suggest a career in music, but rather a love of pronounced rhythms. Latin American music, with its pronounced rhythms and fiery expression is often popular with those who possess this type of thumb.

I noticed the strong angles on my dance teacher's thumbs as he painstakingly taught me to waltz. When I told him I couldn't dance, he sighed and shook his head. Suddenly he grabbed me and together we sailed across the floor, him gliding and me struggling to stay upright, much to his wife's amusement. 'Feel. The. Rhythm. Count … in your head. Feel. The. Rhythm. Count … in your head,' he would say in time to the music. Even now when I hear the music of certain composers I shudder at the memories of stretched tendons and strained muscles from dance lessons.

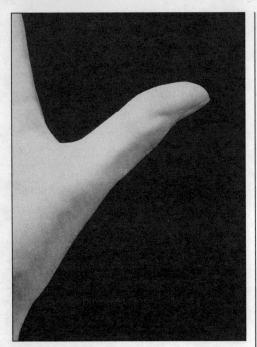

Figure 8 *The stiff thumb*

Stiff thumbs

Stiff thumbs are those which are firm at the first joint; that is, they do not (and cannot) bend backwards. Basically, they are straight, from the second joint (or where the thumb leaves the hand) to the tip of the nail.

People with these thumbs are usually quiet, cautious, economical and practical. They are reserved and undemonstrative with their emotions. They can be plodders, who achieve a little at a time and build their success step by step. They do not easily adapt to new things, and prefer the tried and trusted to the new. They tend to have a strong sense of justice and are self-controlled. They usually weigh up opportunities carefully and demonstrate a practical, commonsense attitude to life. A stiff thumb also indicates a stubborn determination, and these people can be slow to trust new acquaintances.

Stiff-thumbed people are often steady, reliable, and steadfast in friendships, as they respect loyalty. They tend to be loyal to their country and strive to build something lasting, whether it be a home, a business or a nation.

They are usually content with life's offerings and are accepting of their status. As a rule, they complete those things they attempt, which often limits the challenges they undertake. They accept the need for rules and regulations, and enjoy stability and a certain amount of predicability.

Stiff-thumbed people tend to prefer a stable career, such as banking, clerical work, accountancy and engineering.

When involved in an argument, these people stick to their guns and do not back down. I recall interrupting an argument with a friend who has stiff thumbs, because I was laughing so hard that tears were running down my cheeks. In the heat of the moment he had said, 'Oh, you're wrong. You're SO wrong!'

'How wrong is that again?' I asked immediately, and burst into uncontrollable laughter.

The flexible thumb

The flexible thumb is one which can be bent backwards at the first (nail) joint easily. This thumb belongs to those who are often extravagant, impulsive, adaptable and open

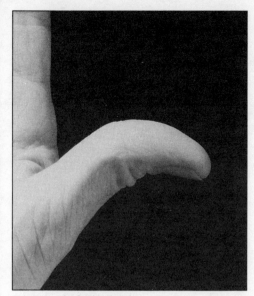

Figure 9 *The flexible thumb*

to new people and opportunities. These people are usually at home almost anywhere. They tend to be sentimental, sympathetic and can be very generous.

Flexible-thumbed people are not inclined to think of the future very much (unless other signs in their hands indicate this) and spend whatever they have financially, emotionally and physically. As a consequence they can be rich one day and poor the next; lively, then exhausted.

The flexibility of their thumbs gives these people a flexibility of mind and of morals. This is not to suggest that this type is immoral, rather that what seems important to them one day may be unimportant the next. They usually achieve great things by fits and starts, but tend to lose interest or become distracted when long-term commitment or repetition is required.

When arguing, these people sometimes tell you what they think you want to hear in order to keep the peace, then they'll happily go and do as they please. Rules and regulations are often given scant attention.

They can fall in love easily and quickly, and out of love every bit as quickly. The same flexibility applies when making friends, moving house, moving country or settling into new work.

Gareth and I were travelling around Ireland for a few weeks. It was July, the height of summer, and it was raining. It had rained the whole four days we had been there, and we were losing hope of ever seeing the sun again. We stopped in a small town for lunch. Gareth was driving, so that meant the stop would consist of three minutes to find a parking space and four minutes to grab a sandwich and a drink.

I couldn't find a sandwich shop anywhere, so I poked my head into a dry-cleaner's to ask directions. The young girl behind the counter had flame red hair and a smile that made up for the miserable day. I fell in love. She told me where to find a bakery, and the shop alongside it was a florist. I returned five minutes later with a bunch of flowers. She blushed nervously and accepted them.

I was in deep trouble when I arrived back at the car some 11 minutes after we had arrived, and when I explained my reasons Gareth choked on his sandwich. 'What? You went out for lunch and you fell in love with the girl in the drycleaner's? You weren't gone long enough to post a letter, let alone fall in love!'

'Look, it's not as foolish as you make it

sound. I merely gave the girl some flowers.'

'You gave her flowers!' he said, shaking his head. I noticed his stiff thumbs and knew that he'd never understand the spontaneity and impulsiveness of my flexible-thumbed approach. His final words made me smile.

'We're leaving town, before her father comes looking for you with a shotgun.'

With flexible-thumbed people, the present moment is far more important than something which lasts until boredom sets in. They do not limit their achievements or maintain the status quo, and as a result they can achieve brilliantly at anything they turn their minds to.

They can often be found in careers which involve a great deal of change or uncertainty, such as acting, the theatre, arts, entertainment and travelling sales positions. When these people work in safe, secure, repetitive jobs, their hands usually show other indications which contradict the thumbs. If not, they will not be too happy at their work for long!

Flexible-thumbed people show adaptability to circumstances. A friend of mine with flexible thumbs compiles a completely new résumé for each job he applies for. On reading a few of these, I could not believe that they were describing the same person. They varied from the complete truth, to part truth, to a litany of lies and fabrications. He doesn't care that he isn't experienced enough for some of the positions, as he plans to learn on the job or leave if the task proves too difficult to master. Aged 36, he has had nearly 40 jobs to date.

KNUCKLES

Prominent knuckles

Swollen or prominent knuckles indicate a slowing down of mental energy. Knotty-fingered people are reflective, and love order and exactness. Prominent upper knuckles (closer to the nail) indicate a love of order in ideas, whereas prominent lower knuckles suggest a love of order in material things.

People with prominent lower knuckles may have a messy desk or room, but in amongst that mess they have a good idea of where things are, and can usually lay their hands on any given thing quickly. Their love of detail helps them focus on tiny things, though they can overlook the obvious.

When making an important decision, it is best for knotty-fingered people to take time to think things over, for in haste they often make poor decisions. A friend of mine with knotty fingers once bought a complete wreck of a car and later confessed that he had fallen in love with the wooden dashboard. Two weeks later he sold it again, having oiled and polished that dashboard. I wondered if he had sold it to another knotty-fingered person?

Smooth fingers

Smooth-fingered people tend to be quick-minded and can become impatient with detail, especially if it is repetitive. They size up a situation quickly and their first impressions are usually correct. They like making quick decisions, so detailed work is best handed to someone else. Smooth fingers can also indicate impulsiveness.

Smooth-fingered Renita and her knotty-fingered mother were shopping for an outfit for Renita. They entered a shop and Renita walked directly towards the clothes rack which appealed to her. She selected one garment and a pair of shoes to match it, and made her way to the counter. Her mother was horrified.

'What about looking around?' she asked.

'Why?'

'Well, you might find something more suitable, or a cheaper outfit.'

Renita reluctantly agreed. They spent the next three hours searching through a dozen boutiques before collapsing in a coffee shop. They decided to give up searching and return home. On their way back they passed the first shop again, and Renita decided to have another look at the first outfit. She loved it, and purchased it immediately.

'You know, Mum, we could have saved an afternoon if you had simply let me buy this when I saw it.'

'How could you buy the first thing you see? At least now you've seen the other outfits and know that you prefer this one.'

THE SIGNIFICANCE OF WEARING RINGS

Rings worn on the fingers and thumbs are significant in palmistry. Electrical (nervous) energy continuously runs down the arms, through the hands and out through the fingertips, and this natural flow of energy is usually impeded when a ring is worn. People often have a problem in a particular area long before they actually start wearing a ring on the corresponding area, and yet the placement of the ring signifies the problem area.

As most rings are composed of gold, which is the best metallic conductor of electricity, or silver, which is the second best, the energy flow is directed around the ring and not down the finger as usual. After several months wearing a ring day and night, the metal effectively isolates the finger from the hand on an energy level. This is not a complete isolation, but it does mean that constantly wearing a ring can isolate some of the qualities that the finger represents. To reverse this, rings need to be removed for approximately five to six months. However, if rings are removed each evening before sleep, the restrictive effect is greatly reduced. The meaning of rings on different fingers is described below.

If you prefer to wear rings, bear in mind that jade, ivory, wood or other non-metal rings do not cause the same restrictions. Also, any ring which does not encircle the whole finger allows more energy to flow naturally to the fingertip.

First finger — Jupiter

Continuously wearing a ring on the Jupiter finger tends to restrict religious or philosophic independence, leaving you searching for someone or something to believe in. People who wear a ring here can show a lack of self-confidence, and they often desire leadership.

Several years ago I knew a woman who

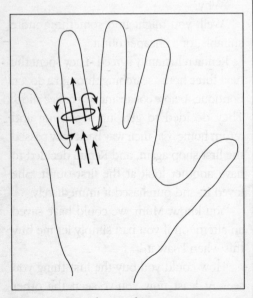

Figure 10 *Rings often impede nervous energy*

wore a ring on this finger, and she was very committed to a religious sect. One day she caught the ring on something and it snapped. Unable to wear it, she placed it in a drawer until she could have it repaired. Twelve months passed and she still had not had her ring repaired. In that time she left the church, and when I asked her why she said, 'It was good, but a bit restrictive. They wouldn't allow for any free thought. I felt a bit stifled at times.'

I met her again three years later and noticed that, once again, she was wearing this ring.

'How's the church?' I asked.

'Oh, good. But how did you know I'd returned?'

'I didn't know, I guessed. Your ring helped.'

Second finger — Saturn

Wearing a ring on the Saturn finger indicates some unresolved conflict or resentment with the father or authority. This unresolved conflict usually continues to the present, appearing as problems with a superior at work, an employer, landlord, partner, police officer, judge, government department and so on. Often the ring wearer finds a partner who repeats this pattern of conflict, or with whom he or she can resolve and overcome any long-term issues. These problems continue to appear in the person's life and hands until the original conflict or resentment is resolved.

I read for a woman who wore a ring on both Saturn fingers. When I mentioned the significance of unresolved issues with her father, she denied any such issues existed. Later I asked her to explain what had happened to an important love relationship ten years ago. I explained that I felt that the relationship had ended but that she had yet to come to terms with her emotions. She stared at me and her eyes widened.

'My father refused to allow me to continue seeing the man I wanted to marry. We separated, and I never saw him again. It was exactly ten years ago this month that we separated.'

Sometimes women with a ring on this finger show contempt for men. Rings on the second finger can also indicate a burning ambition to gain control over yourself and your life. This often manifests itself as an ambition for money or career success. As long as you continue to wear a ring on this finger, you may find yourself being unusually serious or lacking in any desire to be social.

Third finger — Apollo

Wearing a ring on the Apollo finger tends to stifle creativity and originality of expression. The sense of self (or ego boundaries) and independence become restricted. This is often evident when a long-term marriage or relationship breaks down, leaving two 'half people' searching for their 'other half'.

In a relationship, it is necessary to give up a little independence in order to merge with your partner, or to allow yourself to experience what your partner can offer or teach you, yet this needn't impede creativity and originality.

A ring worn on the Apollo finger can also indicate someone who is conscious of his or her ego boundaries within a relationship, because of past experience. Joanne had been single for five years when I noticed the ring on her Apollo finger. 'I'm not in a hurry to get into another relationship just yet. My last one left me without a clear sense of who I am. Before that relationship, I had a large circle of friends, a full life and a job I loved. In 14 years with Andrew I seemed to lose all of that.'

She was developing a sense of herself, and building a circle of friends and personal interests once again.

Fourth finger — Mercury

Wearing a ring on the Mercury finger can reflect difficulties with communication and/or sexual communication. These people easily communicate an idea or philosophy, but rarely reveal their true feelings.

Those who wear a ring here often work in fields where communication is essential; for instance, radio announcers, television presenters, journalists, counsellors, public speakers and salespeople. Close inspection often reveals that their chosen career can be a direct compensation for their inability to communicate on a deeper level.

Thumb

People who wear a ring on their thumbs may, in time, surrender their free will to others, perhaps a partner, a parent or a religious group. Many years ago, when a man married a woman he would place a ring on her thumb, and she would surrender her will to him. She belonged to him.

There has been a resurgence of thumb rings since the 1980s. Though a glance at strangers who wear a thumb ring won't tell you what or whom they surrender their will to, if you examined their life, you'd probably find a person or group controls it.

Another meaning attributed to wearing thumb rings is as follows. I recently read for a woman who wore a ring on her thumb, and had done so for two and a half years. When I questioned her about the change in her life from the time she began wearing this ring, she explained that she had begun seeing a counsellor to help her change her relationship pattern. And the pattern she was trying to change? 'I was tired of men who insisted on dominating me in relationships. They would not allow me to do anything for myself.' Since that time she has been wary of relationships which might repeat that pattern. The fact that she was wearing a ring on her thumb suggested that she was devoting time and attention to the area in question; in this case her free will.

THE NAILS

Moons

The moons in fingernails and thumbnails are the small, milky, crescent shapes at the base of the nails. Moons in thumbnails are larger than those in fingernails and are not included when reading the nails.

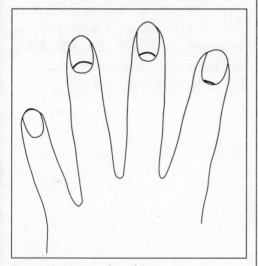

Figure 11 *Moons in the nails*

The size of the moons reflects blood circulation. When the moons are very small or not visible, it indicates poor blood circulation. The symptoms of this are cold hands and feet in cold weather, and the reverse in hot weather.

A large moon (up to one third of the nail) denotes good blood circulation. Southern European and Middle Eastern people usually have large moons. Their enthusiastic approach to life is often assisted by healthy blood circulation.

Regular exercise can improve the blood circulation and, in turn, the size of the moons. A friend of mine has a small baby, and she takes her for two long walks each day. After 14 months of pushing a heavy pram for hours every day, this woman has developed moons which cover one-fifth of her fingernails. Her nails previously showed no moons.

Ridges and flecks

Where there is a sideways ridge (or 'dip') in the nail, it will take approximately six

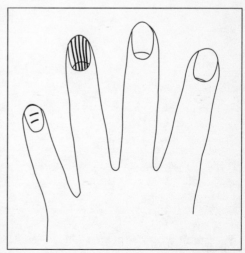

Figure 12 *Ridges in the nails*

months for the ridge to grow from the base of the nail (near the moon) to where the nail no longer contacts the skin. These ridges represent a time in the past six months when health or energy levels were low for a few days or a week, and the nail that was growing at that time was weaker and thinner than usual. This most often happens because of a cold, 'flu, a short illness, shock, trauma, an operation or after an excess intake of alcohol or drugs.

Throughout the first six months of his life, I observed my son's nails, in particular the ridges that had been there since birth (birth can be classified as a shock or a trauma). At five months, the ridges on each of his nails had almost grown out. At seven months, none were visible in any of his nails.

Vertical lines or ridges in the nails can indicate poor absorption of nutrients. This can be due to a poor stomach or poor digestive system. Upward bending nails usually indicate nervous depletion. This type of nail is usually seen on someone who is always 'on the go'. Over a prolonged period, such nervous depletion can lead to a stroke or diseases which affect the nervous system.

White flecks in the nails can denote a lack of calcium and zinc. The physical symptoms can include difficulty with sleeping patterns (an inability to fall asleep easily or a fitful sleep), a short temper or drowsiness immediately after meals. When the body is short of calcium, it often draws it from the nails, bones and teeth.

HAND COLOUR

I was miserable. My jaw hurt from being clenched tight, and the cold found its way through my five layers of clothing to chill my bones. The snow on the platform didn't look so dreamy now that I was its captive. Snow on the tracks meant delays and cancellations, and I was already late.

An old lady appeared at the top step, and made her way slowly to the ticket window. She fumbled in her purse and produced a pension card and two coins. Her hands were thin, frail and blue. The station attendant noticed this and invited her into the ticket room to warm up until the train arrived.

This old woman was cheerful despite the freezing temperature. She had nothing more than a flimsy plastic cover-all, and she would have been 80 years old if she was a day. I had never seen a pair of hands so blue. I kept a close eye on her through the little round window, and she seemed to warm me with her infectious smile and the way she nursed the cup of tea the attendant had given her.

Blue hands are rarely found in temperate climates. They indicate poor blood circulation, often due to a weak heart or a restricted circulatory system. People with blue hands are often self-centred; they have insufficient energy and vitality for them-selves, let alone any spare energy for others.

Red hands indicate surplus energy and great vitality, and often are a sign of high blood pressure. People with red hands tend to do too many things at once. A red tinge under the nails also indicates high blood pressure. White skin under the nails usually indicates low blood pressure.

Yellow hands indicate that too much bile is being pumped into the body by the liver. This excess bile finds its way into the blood stream, becoming a toxin or poison in the blood. This taxes the body of energy, as the body seeks to rid itself of this toxin. The most obvious place for the blood to deposit this liquid is in the cells and the skin, hence the skin turns yellow. This mild poisoning can contribute to short-temperedness.

If the skin under the nails is yellow, the condition is longstanding one, and will be difficult to reverse. In such cases, see a qualified medical or alternative practitioner for a more accurate diagnosis. If the skin under the nails is pink, then the condition could be in its early stages, and early intervention can bring positive results.

Pink hands indicate a well-balanced physical body, and these are the hands most often seen. These people recover from ill-ness quickly, and they usually bounce back from emotional setbacks.

WARTS

Warts usually represent anger and their placement on the hand indicates what the anger is related to. When a wart is located on one of the mounts it signifies resentment associated with the qualities of that mount (see Part III). The placement of warts and their corresponding meanings are as follows:

- **Jupiter finger or mount:** anger or resentment about an inability to pursue a chosen ambition, career or philosophy.
- **Saturn finger or mount:** resentment about restrictions in your life, about the father, or about the lack of a father during childhood.

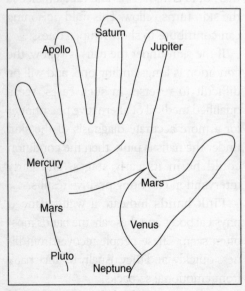

Figure 13 *Warts on the hands*

- **Apollo finger or mount:** creative frustration.
- **Mercury finger or mount:** frustration in communication or in business.
- **Thumb:** anger or resentment at not being able to exercise free will in certain situations.
- **Mount of Mars under Mercury:** resentment about others opposing your plans.
- **Mount of Luna:** frustration with the mother figure, or lack of time to daydream, or insecurity in childhood.
- **Mount of Pluto:** deep anger or resentment, probably present since birth, relating to personal power and an inability to surrender to life. It can signify resentment resulting from a sense of powerlessness.
- **Mount of Neptune:** resentment about not being able to dream, to dance, to paint or to follow a spiritual path.
- **Mount of Venus:** anger at a partner, lover or an ex-partner.
- **Mount of Mars under Jupiter:** anger at being unable to start something, or to be free of rigid discipline.

Karen was eight years old when her mother first noticed the warts on her hands. There were nine of them, and within a month there were fifteen. She took Karen to the family doctor. The doctor asked to speak to Karen alone for five minutes and, when they were alone, he offered to buy all her warts for an agreed price. They talked for a while and finally Karen agreed to sell them to him. He paid her half the money and made an appointment for her to see him again in eight weeks.

By the time she returned to the doctor, all her warts had disappeared. She had undergone no treatment, therapy or ritual to remove them. The doctor smiled when he saw her, and gladly paid her the other half of the money. This particular doctor believed that, more often than not, warts have emotional or mental causes, and his unusual method of treatment proved him to be correct in this case.

TEXTURE OF PALMS

The texture of palms, whether moist or dry, firm or soft, is of great significance in palmistry. I often hear the argument that the type of work people do will determine how moist their hands become, but this is not so. I rarely do any manual work and yet I have firm, dry hands. Those who do a great deal of manual work can develop callused hands, but except for the actual calluses, the palms remain as they are; either moist or dry, firm or soft.

People with dry palms tend to be intellectual and are more likely to approach life through their mind and their thoughts. Moist-handed people are lovers of luxury and indolence (especially when the palm is soft) and relate to the world through feelings and touch.

I once shook hands with a large, well-built man who seemed an athletic and outdoors type. However, his cold, clammy hands suggested the opposite. These soft, moist hands belonged to an indulgent and somewhat indolent person. They were the hands of someone who prefers comfort to exercise, or to dream and talk of adventure rather than to experience adventure directly.

The stories he told of his experiences in China in the 1950s intrigued me, but I couldn't help wondering if these adventures were his own, or remembered from a book or a friend. A tall woman approached us and interrupted our conversation. 'Oh David, you're not telling tall stories about the East again are you? Don't believe a word of it, Paul.' Saying this, she took his arm and led him away into the crowd.

There is little chance of hiding yourself behind a deliberately firm handshake when your soft, moist hands give you away anyway.

Firm hands show an energetic person, one who bounces back from illness quickly and easily. **Soft hands** show someone who is not so inclined to physical pursuits, but instead seeks out comfort and security. In short, the firm-handed person climbs the mountain, and the soft-handed person serves them a drink in the bar at the mountain's peak.

HAIR ON THE HANDS

Hair on the back of the hands reveals further information about your personality. **Dark hair** indicates a volatile temperament and a strong character. **Red hair** indicates an excitable nature and increases the enthusiasm with which these people approach life. **Blonde hair** denotes a less volatile but rather sulky temperament. These people tend to be cool with their emotions.

The more hair there is on the hands, the more energy you have. Where you use this energy is shown by the mounts and the palms generally.

In Chinese palmistry, hair on the hands is believed to indicate a primitive or unevolved nature, as most Chinese do not have hair on the backs of their hands. In Greek palmistry, hair on the hands of a man is accepted as a sign of masculinity and a lack of hair is considered feminine.

DIVISIONS OF ENERGY

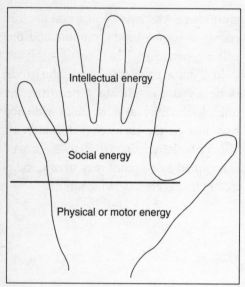

Intellectual energy

Social energy

Physical or motor energy

Figure 14 *Divisions of energy*

The hand can be divided into three sections, each of which indicates how we approach life:

1. From the base of the fingers to the fingertips, represents intellectual energy. This area is usually prominent in hands with long fingers and/or full, fleshy pads on the fingertips.
2. Where the thumb leaves the hand to the base of the fingers represents emotional or social energy. Prominent social energy is shown by full, fleshy pads or mounts directly under the fingers.
3. The lower part of the palm, from the wrist to where the thumb leaves the hand represents physical or motor energy. Prominence in this area is shown by full, fleshy pads or mounts below the thumb and across the base of the hand.

A quick look at people's hands can indicate where their energy is prominent or deficient. If they show prominent energy in the lower part of the palm, it is likely they tend towards sports and physical exercise. They often judge something by how they feel about it and what it feels like to touch. They may need to touch a person or thing to fully understand it. They are the type who, when pointing to an object inside a shop window or on a computer screen, must touch the window or screen. Theirs is a kinaesthetic approach to life.

Those with prominent energy in the middle section tend to spend much of their time socialising or communicating with others. They are often better suited to work which involves people. When making an important decision, they are likely to take into account how others around them feel. If they work without other people around them, they often use the phone to keep in touch with friends and colleagues.

People with prominent energy in the fingers have a more intellectual grasp of things. They are fascinated by thoughts and ideas, books and learning. They love to discuss life's possibilities and abstract ideas. When making an important decision, they like to discuss the alternatives with anyone who will listen or offer an opinion.

When I was reading Roger's hands, he spent much of the time explaining how he loved to research and invent new software programs for computers, and how he was constantly being frustrated by the other company directors, who wanted him to put more energy into the sales and marketing of the products. 'I try to explain the possibilities contained within my work, but they just don't seem to be interested,' he lamented. His long fingers with their long first phalanges showed him to be much more interested in understanding possibilities than the realities of market share or sales figures.

The ancient Greeks believed that when a child was born, the energy required to release the baby into life was channelled through the baby's hand, in particular through the two first fingers, where it would rush up the arms and into the body. This energy transfer was supposed to take only one or two seconds, and anything that impeded this energy transfer would mean the child had less physical energy or vitality. The things that could slow down this energy included prominent knuckles, a thin hand, and narrow fingers and nails. As this energy flowed more freely through a wider hand, wider hands indicated a more energetic person.

WHICH HAND SHOULD
BE READ?

He was standing on a stage, with the hot lights obscuring his view of the audience, as he routinely and mechanically went through the motions of the play for the ninety-seventh time. He knew this scene backwards, and had been saying these lines in his sleep for the past three weeks. Suddenly an idea leapt into his conscious mind. His eyes widened at the possibilities.

'Change the script,' his mind screamed, 'and while you're at it, change your accent and the mood of this tedious piece. Liven it up a little. At least it will keep the other players on their toes. At best it will entertain both the audience and yourself.'

He tried to subdue his mind, but it would not be diverted. As he delivered the same old lines as yesterday, his mind formed a plan to burst into song towards the close of the scene. Would he dare risk a bleak future of hunger and unemployment, or was he to die a little each night, before a room full of witnesses?

He burst forth with an old naval song, and the startled looks from his fellow actors only served to make him more determined. He winked at the actor facing him and, to his surprise, that actor and another joined in his song. They formed a perfect three-part harmony, and the audience was unaware of their little embellishment of the original play. There were six weeks of variations ahead of them; variations on this original theme. The play was now a challenge instead of a tedious chore.

Your original life path is shown in your non-writing hand. Some people make few or no changes to the original script, so both their hands appear similar. Others set about improving or diminishing what awaits them, and the hands of these people vary considerably from left to right.

Your non-writing hand can be likened to the original script of a play, while your writing hand resembles the changes you make to the script. Your crazy antics, your spontaneous songs and your improvements on the original play of your life are shown in your writing hand.

One approach is not better than another, merely different. If you are fatalistic, you will probably be only too happy to follow your destiny to its conclusion and not change anything that is written in your hands. You might consider this as being faithful to your original purpose. If you believe in free will, you will probably have already altered what was originally written for you. You are likely to be continually examining your options and the possible futures which could result from your current decisions.

The act of writing, or favouring a hand, gives that hand more contact with the brain than the other one, and the lines on the palm change in accordance with the new direction being followed. This hand details the future. It also explains why the non-writing hand, which changes more slowly, gives more detail about the past and original potential — what life held in store for us before we exercised free will.

In rare cases, I have found that the right hands of left-handed people still foretell the future. I believe this is because some left-handed people were encouraged or even pressured to use their right hand for all tasks other than writing.

If in doubt as to which hand will be more accurate with the future, I simply read dates and events from the person's past, first from one hand and then the other. Whichever hand gives more accurate information about the recent past is the hand of the future.

Part II
Types of
hands

SPATULATE HANDS

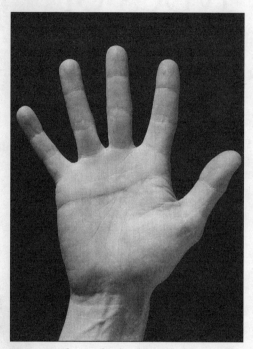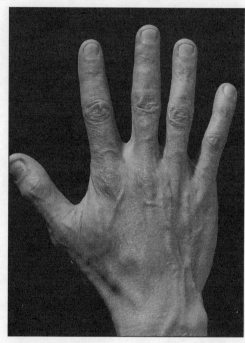

Figure 15 *The spatulate hand (note the triangular-shaped nails and knotty fingers)*

Spatulate hands are so called because the fingertips often resemble a chemist's spatula. This is a wide hand, usually quite firm, with almost triangular nails. The nails are always wider at the tip than at the base. There is often plenty of space between the fingers, even when relaxed on the table, palm downwards.

People with spatulate hands are sceptical, scientific and analytical, so when reading for them it is important to explain how you are finding the information that you give to them. Spatulate-handed people generally love freedom, space, travel, change, independence, challenge, competition and to know how things work. They like to take things apart to see what makes them tick. They are very often inventive. They can be very enthusiastic about trying out their ideas, which tend to be either brilliant or disastrous. These people require proof. When faced with the science of palmistry, they either ridicule the method or demand an explanation. If you can present your case clearly and give accurate evidence, those with spatulate hands often want to learn this science for themselves.

A spatulate hand can be broadest at the base of the fingers or at the wrists. Spatulate-handed people whose hands are broadest at the base of the fingers tend to be fascinated with ideas, concepts and thoughts. They enjoy analysing people and if they invent something it is likely to be conceptual, philosophical or theoretical.

If their hands are broadest at the wrist, they love to take apart real things, such as cars, vacuum cleaners and machinery. When this type invents something, it will often be practical, tangible and useful. I have a friend with these hands who cannot resist taking apart anything which breaks down. Unfortunately, he has a short attention span, so very few things he dismantles are ever seen in one piece again. When he visits I insist that everything is in perfect working order and ensure that anything that is not working is well hidden.

The easiest way to seek out spatulate-handed types is to find a group of active people. They are often found at sports fields, athletic events, martial arts schools, competitive sporting events and working at construction sites or as adventure tour guides. Spatulate hands denote an enthusiastic nature, and this type of person needs plenty of outdoor activity. If continuously confined, they stir up trouble simply for some excitement. Without healthy competition, they may seek out a battle.

A spatulate hand can indicate a scientific bent, but these people usually display dynamic energy, preferring to act rather than observe. With soft, moist hands, however, they may dream and plan adventures without actually acting on their plans. The softness of the hands has taken away the physical energy needed to put plans into action. However, soft spatulate hands are uncommon. Prominent knuckles are common on spatulate hands and show a need to analyse.

'How can you prove that it really works, that it's not just fortune telling?' came a voice from the crowd gathered around my market stall. I glanced up in search of a perfect pair of spatulate hands which remained hidden. A bearded man in the second row met my eyes with a challenge, and I decided to play along with him.

'Would you agree, sir, that I have not examined your hands?' I asked him loudly.

'Yes, I could safely say that,' came the reply.

'And would you be prepared to hold an open mind on the subject of palmistry if I could accurately describe the shape of your fingernails and your hands without looking at them?'

'Perhaps.'

'Perhaps,' I repeated, and feigned disinterest.

'Okay, I would,' he stated for all to hear.

'Fine. You have broad, firm hands with wide spaces between the fingers and triangular or fan-shaped nails. The nails are short and are wider than they are long. You have prominent or knotty knuckles on the lower joints.'

There was silence as the onlookers

gathered around the man's hands to check my description. He was not convinced.

'That is a very general description. It could describe anyone's hands.'

'Oh. Add to that a pair of stiff thumbs,' I laughed, and held up my flexible thumbs to show the crowd what I meant. The murmuring grew louder, and I noticed the man examining his hands carefully as I returned to my client's hands on the table.

The spatulate-handed man sat down for a reading some 40 minutes later, and at the close of his session he stated, 'It's an interesting theory, but I'm not completely convinced.' I gave him my card and he left.

Three weeks later I received a call from him. He asked me a few deep questions about palmistry — he had obviously been reading up on the subject. He told me that he was almost through his third book.

'You're well on your way to becoming a palmist, too,' I said.

'Not quite. It's an interesting theory, but I'm not completely convinced yet.'

CONIC HANDS

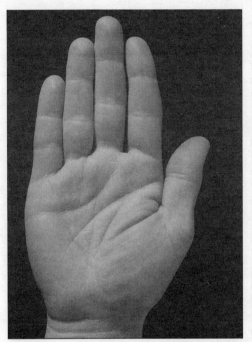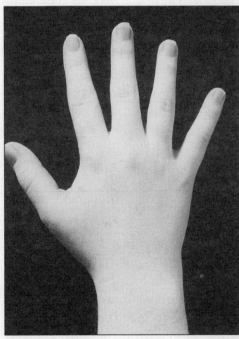

Figure 16 *The conic hand (note the rounded nails and the low-set Mercury finger)*

Conic hands are the most common type of hands and are shaped a little like a pine cone. The fingers have rounded nails, which are oval or almond shaped. Conic hands usually have smooth fingers; that is, the fingers will be smooth from tip to base. As the knuckles are not prominent, the fingers tend to look longer than they actually are.

Conic-handed people are usually impulsive, intuitive and often have short attention spans. They tend to go through phases with friends, partners, fashion, food and work — in fact, almost everything in their lives. I can count on at least one conic-handed person phoning for a place in one of my courses at short notice.

'Hello. I hear you have a palmistry course starting on Sunday.'

'Yes, that's right.'

'Are there any available places left?'

'I think it's completely booked up at this late stage, but I have another course beginning in 12 weeks if you're interested.'

'Oh, I couldn't wait that long. I don't

know what I'll be doing then. Are you sure there isn't one place?'

'I'll take your name and number and see what I can arrange.'

Conic-handed people are generally at their best with strangers, as they enjoy meeting new people and having varied conversations, and easily tire of repetitive situations. They tend to flow with the mood of the moment more than any other type. They begin many more things than they complete, as new and more promising things lure them away.

A friend with conic hands is a classic (if extreme) example of the type. In the first ten weeks I knew her, she changed her hair colour five times (black, blonde, red, blue-black and, finally, sky blue) before it all fell out because it had been bleached too often. Meanwhile, she had two jobs, two boyfriends and was toying with changing her name. When accompanying her in public, I would be included in a few unusual conversations with the most unlikely people. Her friends included priests, prostitutes, drug dealers, politicians, artists, business people and almost everyone in between.

Conic hands with prominent knuckles present a contradiction. There is the impulsiveness of the type, added to which is a love of detail and analysis. It indicates a person who is both impulsive *and* analytical.

With a Conic hand, the Mercury finger is usually set lower than the others. This gives the base of the fingers (when looking at the palms) a bow shape. Conic-handed people do not often find success in business

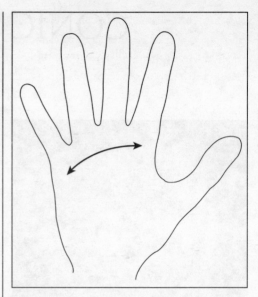

Figure 17 *Conic hands usually have low-set Mercury fingers*

unless with a partner, or unless the business involves a great deal of variety. This is because the Mercury (or business) finger is set lower than the others, which reduces its effectiveness and therefore the person's business ability.

Harmony is very important to conic-handed people. When there is disharmony around them they usually sense it immediately, and often take it upon themselves to try to balance the situation; for instance, by settling a dispute or distracting those concerned by starting a new conversation.

Novelty and sensation appeal to these types. They are suited to careers in magazine publishing, television and the entertainment industry because of their short attention spans and demand for constant change. Conic-handed people are often so busy beginning a new project that their interest wanes in completing what is already in progress. Teamed with a square-handed person, the conic-handed person easily begins something and the square-handed usually completes it.

Small conic hands with smooth fingers indicate very quick thoughts and impulsiveness. These people are best suited to careers where ideas are required, such as the advertising industry, media, television, film making, fashion and the service industries, including hairdressing, hotel reception and sales positions.

Conic-handed people are the ones with garages filled with creative tools which mark the various phases they have been through — a spinning wheel, a set of weight-training equipment, a potter's wheel, an easel and some paints, a porcelain painting set, a course on how to write a best seller, a few musical instruments, a yoga mat, candle-making equipment and even a few flower pots, complete with the dried-up remains of plants. The conic-handed person's garage sale is one not to be missed!

SQUARE HANDS

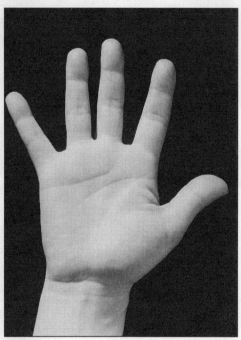
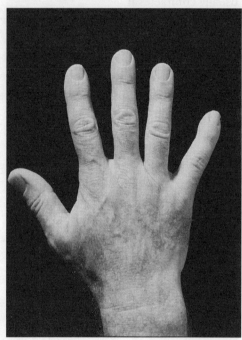

Figure 18 *The square hand (note that the fingers are set evenly on a line, and the square or rectangular palm)*

'It is a good idea, and certainly original, but don't you think it would be better to tone it down a little? Is it possible that it might reach a wider audience and buying public if it were aimed a little more squarely at the average person?'

What could I say? He was right of course, and he was also the man with the money to finance the project.

I swallowed hard and thought for a moment. It was two years since we had given birth to what we felt was the most original idea for a board game. Eric and I had worked on this project late into the night for 18 of those 24 months. All the nights spent cutting and pasting, all the hasty trips to the printers, all the researching of patents and trade marks and all the trials with friends and strangers had not prepared me for the man with square hands who had the power to give our project the finance we believed it deserved.

It was original. It was also outrageous, shocking and lurid in both colour and content; the sort of thing a square-handed person would prefer to avoid.

'Exactly how would you tone it down?' I asked when I could summon the courage. His suggestions were practical, sensible and reasonable, and allowed the original concept to remain intact.

In a square hand the palm is square at the wrist, square at the base of the fingers (all the fingers are set evenly on a line) and the fingers are also square. Even the nails usually have straight sides and are square or rectangular in shape.

Square-handed people do not like change, preferring familiarity. They tend to respect authority and like discipline. They can be very methodical in their work, their habits and in their thinking processes. They tend to be moderate people, in tastes and in travel, often travelling to the same place each year for holidays. In religious and philosophic beliefs they can lack flexibility, preferring instead rigid belief systems.

These types are usually practical, conservative, punctual and orderly. They form habits quickly, and they do not like to deviate from them. This type often has difficulty sleeping when on holiday, because the bed is unfamiliar or because they 'always sleep by the window', and they often bring their own pillows with them.

They tend not to adapt well to new people and new ideas, having limited originality or imagination. In their work they can often be very successful due to their tenacity, application and strength of will. They are usually reliable and finish what they begin, partly because they do not start what they are unsure of finishing and also because they enjoy practical projects.

Square-handed people tend not to question as much as spatulate types, nor do they seek novelty as conic types do. They enjoy knowing their limitations and are content to work within a set boundary. They are often staunch in friendship, strong in principle and honest in business. Fairness is important to square-handed people. They have more difficulty in adjusting to anything new or different, and are more comfortable with a mundane environment than the other types are.

A square hand with long fingers denotes a person who is materialistic, scientific, cautious and thoroughly logical and reasonable. With short, square fingers, this type can be very materialistic, narrow-minded and obstinate. They seek wealth and only tend to believe in what they can see and touch.

Square-handed people with prominent (knotty) knuckles show a great love of detail. Given a starting point and a destination, this type carefully works out the details necessary to get from A to B. These people are keen to know all the ins and outs of the career they pursue, and are suited to architecture, business, mathematics, computer work, medical or scientific work.

Even when in creative careers, square-handed people prefer a practical approach. They are the method actors, the musicians who diligently practise and the painters who spend five years honing their skills in oils before commencing with watercolours. It is interesting to note that although conic-handed people are the artistic types, those with square hands are more likely to be recognised for their artistic endeavours. This is due to their tenacity and the practical application of their talents. If you require a reliable product or service, a square-handed person is most likely to give it to you. A mechanic with square hands is usually thorough, and a square-handed tailor, precise.

I saw the work of my dentist long before I was his client. A friend confided to me one day that three of her front teeth were the product of this dentist, as she had broken them one night while attempting to remove the cork from a bottle of wine. He had rebuilt her teeth to a standard I did not believe possible.

During my first appointment I noticed that the dentist had long, knotty fingers on a pair of spatulate hands with square thumbs, and I knew that all the details would be taken into consideration. It is no easy feat to read your dentist's hands as he delves into your mouth!

Spatulate fingers increase square-handed people's ability to invent practical things. Mechanical things appeal to them and they are likely to invent something useful for around the house. They can be every bit as successful as spatulate types where invention is concerned, as they possess a patience that spatulate types do not. If something doesn't work the first time, they usually try again.

A square hand with conic fingers is the mark of a recognised artist. Although the artist's hand technically belongs in the conic category, the true artist is content never to put a pen to paper, a paintbrush to canvas, or a piece of music on paper. The conic-handed artist loves beauty for beauty's sake and, in savouring the moment, experiences no desire to capture the feeling in any permanent form. Thus the square hand with conic fingers combines the practical, persevering nature of the square type with the artistic appreciation of the conic type. The application and continuity of effort required to perfect technique are not possessed by the conic hand and the artistic inspiration and appreciation are not characteristics of the square hand. Combining the two qualities gives these people enough imagination to inspire them and enough application to see them through to completion of a creative project.

A square hand with psychic fingers is rare. It is a blend of two types that are so completely different from one another that these people begin something with every good intention, only to lose hope or mood or purpose. Consequently they complete very little of what they begin. They understand the practical and the spiritual, but have difficulty reconciling them.

I have seen this combination in a Chinese woman, Anna, who had a pure psychic left hand and a square right hand with psychic fingers. She was trying very hard to fit into the Western way of life. She would become distressed even in the most normal and routine situations.

We worked together in a large hotel. Anna was the front office manager and it was her duty to organise guest registrations and to see that everything ran smoothly. Every Sunday at 4.15 pm, two busloads of weary tourists would arrive to be checked in. Yet every Sunday at 4.00 pm Anna would be sitting quietly, drinking coffee and staring out into space. At the sound of the bus she would panic. Within two minutes the foyer would be knee-deep in duty free purchases and shoulder-deep in tourists wanting a bed, a bath and a change of clothes.

One Sunday, a different woman was working Anna's shift, and at 4.00 pm she was lining up 50 registration forms on the check-in desk to speed up the process. The guests were processed in half the time, and with less than half the stress.

Square-handed people with mixed fingers can be inventive, creative, inspirational and practical. It is an adaptable combination, for the variety of fingers adds to the flexibility, but these people often do not succeed due to a lack of continuity of purpose. They may try too many projects, or too many approaches to a problem to be able to see something through to its completion.

PHILOSOPHIC HANDS

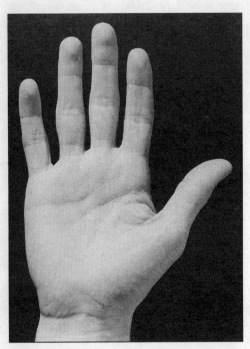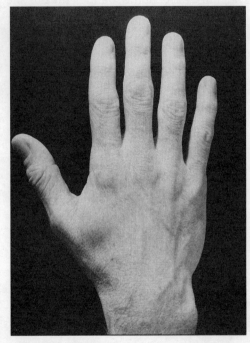

Figure 19 *The philosophic hand (note the long, bony, rectangular palm and the long, knotty fingers)*

Philosophy in direct translation refers to a love of wisdom. It derives from the Greek words *philos* — love — and *sophia* — wisdom. The philosophic hand is long and angular, with bony fingers, knotty knuckles and long fingernails.

These people prefer wisdom and understanding to material things. Philosophy and psychology — in fact, any study of humankind — interests these people keenly. They tend to see themselves as different or distinct from other people, and

are prepared to go to great lengths to ensure that this is so. They have a thirst for knowledge and, as knowledge can give power, they have a power over other people, not material things.

Damian was ten minutes early for his appointment and, because I was finishing lunch, I asked him to wait in my office. When I entered the room, I found him deeply engrossed in a book on spiritual masters of India, and he had a further three books on the table next to him. After I read his hands, he produced a pen and paper and listed five books and their authors.

'Perhaps I came today for some reading of a different sort,' he mused as he placed a large volume on spiritual practices back on the shelf.

'Always learning, always observing,' I thought to myself. The philosophic hand in its essence.

Philosophic-handed people tend to look beyond the meeting of their immediate needs, beyond survival, to seek a purpose for existence. They seek their own place in the universe and humanity's place in the cosmic scheme of things. Because of this, they tend to be drawn towards the church and philosophic groups, such as the Brahmans of India and the Buddhist monks of Thailand. Philosophic-handed people can be found at alternative bookshops, meditation and yoga courses, libraries, engrossed in a book at a party, managing a stall at a market in support of a particular cause, or taking part in a religious discussion.

In character, these people tend to be silent, deep thinkers and careful in their choice of words. In their actions they are careful to demonstrate their differences from the rest of humanity.

A friend of mine has an eight-year-old son with philosophic hands who seems to disdain his family, finding them ordinary and beneath him. When he visited my home he was fascinated by the fact that I rarely went out of the house to work, and that between clients I play the piano or water the garden. My work seemed to him to be secondary to my life, and he decided that he wanted his adult years to be the same.

It was a great relief for him to find that being an adult didn't mean having to work nine to five. This same boy asked his religious education teacher, 'If a person doesn't believe in God, will he still go to heaven?' The teacher had replied that it was a very good question, but tactfully avoided answering it.

Those with philosophic hands patiently wait for opportunities, and thus they are more aware of an opportunity's potential when it arrives. They analyse past actions and learn from experience. Their desire is to understand humanity and to understand themselves.

In their pursuit of truth, they are often prepared to make sacrifices and undergo self-deprivation in order to attain the knowledge or goals they seek. They possess the patience of the square-handed type and the love of exploration of the conic-handed type, which makes them suitable to a religious, monastic or mystical life.

As philosophic-handed people do not greatly value material things, they rarely rise to great heights according to the standards set by average people. A woman with philosophic hands recently consulted me for a tarot reading. One of her questions was, 'Am I going to be financially well off?' I puzzled aloud why she would be so interested in money matters and she laughed. 'Oh, I'm not. My friend in the waiting room insisted that I ask, and she wants to hear the tape, so I thought I'd better ask.' Her friend had square hands.

Philosophic types are aware of their innate need for knowledge and understanding, which sets them apart from the average person. They tend to spend their time in search of that which no one can hold, own or use in the physical world, for they know that if you cannot take it with you, it is of little value.

In my palmistry courses I often tell the following story to illustrate the philosophic type.

A philosophic-handed man climbs the highest mountain, taking a conic-handed person part of the way to enjoy the scenery. On his way, the philosophic man meets a spatulate type who is making the most of the great outdoors. The spatulate-handed man ignores the path, preferring to scale the sheer cliff face using ropes and tackle equipment supplied by a square-handed person, for these are the safest.

Long after the philosophic-handed man has left the others behind, the air becomes thin and clear, and he meets with the object of his search. He meets his guru; the man with psychic hands. They talk for a while, and then the philosophic-handed man returns to the plains in order to reflect upon their conversation.

DIFFERENT TYPES OF HANDS

Spatulate hands	These people are 'doers', always on the go.
Conic hands	These people love change, entertainment and are impatient and spontaneous.
Square hands	These people are logical, practical and cautious.
Philosophic hands	These people desire knowledge and an understanding of humankind. They are also thoughtful.
Psychic hands	These people need encouragement, for if pushed too far they will retreat into themselves. They are sensitive, creative and spiritual in their approach to life.
Broader/larger hands	These people have a great deal of physical energy.
Small hands	These people have little physical energy, but high mental energy.

PSYCHIC HANDS

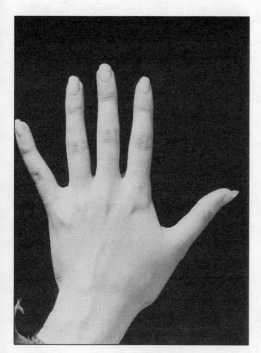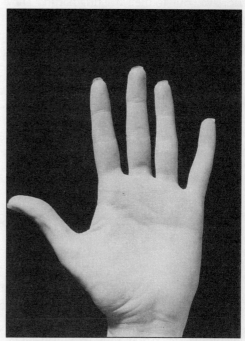

Figure 20 *The psychic hand (note the smooth, tapering fingers and long, narrow palm)*

'My children laugh about my hands. They say that these are the hands of a witch,' she said apologetically as she placed a pair of thin, bony, long-fingered hands on the table. They were as delicate as she appeared to be. I guessed that her children teased her because she wouldn't fight back. She had classic psychic hands.

The pure type of psychic hands is rarely found, particularly in the West. It is a long, narrow hand, with delicate long fingers and long, almond-shaped nails. The fingers are always smooth. The narrowness of the hand indicates a lack of physical vitality and a more passive nature than the other types. These people have an intellectual approach to the spiritual side of life.

Psychic-handed people possess an idealistic nature. They appreciate the inner beauty of all things, seeking not to disturb the equilibrium but rather to observe the flow of life towards its real purpose.

These people are gentle, kind and caring to all those who need help and, as such, are often taken for granted or abused by those who relate a sad story to enlist their pity. They trust those who are kind to them and are usually unsuited to business, being essentially impractical. They can be easily deceived due to their trusting nature. They deeply resent this, and repeated disappointment finds them withdrawing into themselves and their minds. This is not to suggest they are foolish or unintelligent, simply that from their perspective, the smaller things can have as much meaning as the larger things.

To simplify, those with psychic hands are *in* this world but not *of* this world. They know that, in the end, none of what we gather can be taken with us, and that desires and accumulated things only hold us back. Theirs is a life of detachment. Consciously or not, they are religious by nature, attracted to magic and mystery. They are often naturally intuitive and need to avoid much of life's negativity. They make good mediums, clairvoyants and psychic readers, although this drains their limited energy supplies.

Psychic-handed people are not suited to manual work, business or any career that involves competition, for defeat makes them reclusive and afraid to try again. They need constant encouragement and, if encouraged, can demonstrate a rare talent for painting, poetry, writing and dreaming. They can often be found in careers which involve caring for the aged, in hospitals and hospices, as well as working in animal shelters or animal rescue stations. Religious and philosophic orders also appeal to them, but unlike philosophic-handed types, they rely more on faith than understanding.

Psychic types often cannot see the point in struggling to survive when there are dreams to be dreamed. The material world demands real, tangible things of each of us and these people often feel that they have little to offer. They do, however, for when all the work is done and when all our needs are met, who else will remind us of our true purpose on this earth?

Alexandra came to one of my classes so the students could examine her perfectly psychic hands. During our reading, I sensed that very few people in Alexandra's life had actually listened to her, understood her, or seen what she had to offer as valuable. Her long hands, and the lines on her palms, showed a life of brutal treatment from those who were responsible for her safe conduct into adulthood. Her careless guardians delivered her into the arms of life, a crushed and broken woman. Her husband continued the ill treatment for the next 17 years.

It took a further 21 years to redress some of the damage he caused, and now, at 61, Alexandra is deaf, almost blind, has poor balance and high blood pressure. Only chemicals keep her ill health under control. She struggles to understand why all this occurred and what purpose it has served. I wanted to convey to her that I understood her pain and suffering, that she is too sensitive for the life she was given, but all I could say was, 'Life has not been kind to you, it seems'. Her eyes met mine, and for a moment we shared her pain, together.

Part III
Character traits —
the mounts of the hand

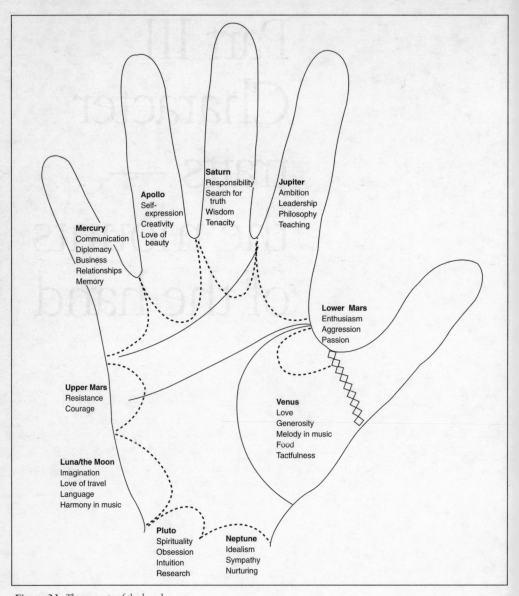

Mercury
Communication
Diplomacy
Business
Relationships
Memory

Apollo
Self-
expression
Creativity
Love of
beauty

Saturn
Responsibility
Search for
truth
Wisdom
Tenacity

Jupiter
Ambition
Leadership
Philosophy
Teaching

Lower Mars
Enthusiasm
Aggression
Passion

Upper Mars
Resistance
Courage

Venus
Love
Generosity
Melody in music
Food
Tactfulness

Luna/the Moon
Imagination
Love of travel
Language
Harmony in music

Pluto
Spirituality
Obsession
Intuition
Research

Neptune
Idealism
Sympathy
Nurturing

Figure 21 *The mounts of the hand*

The mounts of the hand are the fleshy pads below the fingers and around the edge of the palm. Each mount is named after a planet and each one details certain characteristics.

Many books on palmistry devote little space to the mounts, as they are considered by some to be unimportant. When you have to give a full reading to someone who has only three lines on each palm, however, you will discover how important the mounts are. They detail personality type, interests, approach to life and health tendencies.

The purpose of studying the mounts so carefully is that, with practice, you will be able to judge which mount is prominent on someone's hand by observing the person's size, shape and build, and the size and placement of the eyes, ears and nose. In other words, you'll have a pretty good idea about a person's character before you even look at his or her hands.

I have a scrapbook of photographs of famous people with their hands up to the camera. When a film or rock star doesn't want to be photographed, they seem to give us their hands to read instead. The outstretched palm with its lines clearly visible is a common position for famous people seeking a little privacy from the paparazzi. A curious palmist never wastes an opportunity to view a pair of hands. It is interesting what you can learn.

For a mount to be prominent, it needs to be full and firm or, in the case of Saturn and Apollo, marked with a vertical line. The corresponding finger should be long, straight and independent of the others; that is, it should not lean towards another finger.

The following descriptions of the mounts are for pure types, or for hands which have one prominent mount and no opposing secondary mount. People with this type of hand are rare. Most hands are a combination of several types, with one prominent mount and a secondary mount which adds finer detail to the description of the subject's character. Many people also have a third well-developed mount, which gives even more detail about their character, likes, dislikes and so on.

As well as pure types, there are negative (or spoiled) types. The pure type displays most of the qualities of the type, whereas the negative type exhibits predominantly negative traits. Such things as crooked fingers and large crosses, chains or grilles on the mount indicate a negative type.

SIGNS ON THE MOUNTS

Squares: A square on a mount gives protection, and the protection offered varies according to the mount upon which it is found. The exception to this is the Mount of Venus, where a square details a period of physical or emotional imprisonment which has already occurred.

Triangles: A triangle on a mount indicates great mental focus and is always a positive sign. Ensure that it is not a chance crossing of lines, for a triangle formed in this way shows less mental brilliance than an independent triangle.

Dots: A dot on a mount is a sign that its normal energy flow is interrupted slightly, according to the size and number of dots present.

Grilles: A grille (a net-like criss-cross of lines) on a mount has the effect of tying down or repressing the qualities of the mount. This, in turn, leads to the negative qualities of the mount leaking out of the 'net' or grille, increasing the negative tendencies of the mount.

Circles: A circle is rarely found on the palm and refers to trouble with the eyes if found on the lines of Life or Heart. In some cases, it suggests that the person's life was 'going around in circles' at the time when the circle appeared on the line.

Crosses: An independent cross (not a chance crossing of lines) found on a mount represents an obstacle or a defeat that will adversely affect the person's life. It can signify an inability to channel the energies of the mount effectively; for instance, a cross on the Mount of Mars would detail difficulties in channelling anger or aggression into some worthwhile purpose.

Single vertical lines: A single vertical line on a mount increases the positive qualities of that mount. Ensure that the line is not one of the main lines, such as the lines of Fate and Sun on the mounts of Saturn and Apollo.

THE MOUNT OF JUPITER

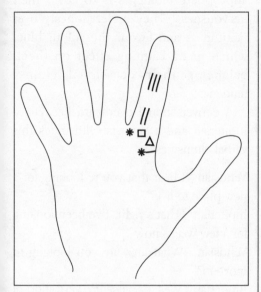

Figure 22 *Lines and signs on the Mount of Jupiter*

Jupiter is the mount under the first finger. When it is full and firm, with a straight, independent finger, and clearly the prominent mount of the hand, the person can be described as Jupiterian.

Jupiterians are usually medium to tall in height and of strong build, with large, expressive eyes. They tend to be fleshy. When Jupiterian women put on weight, it is usually disproportionately placed on the hips, thighs and buttocks. The men tend to be quite hairy. They perspire easily, especially around the forehead, and in men this can lead to premature baldness. The hair is usually thick, strong and wavy. They

often have a dimpled chin, and the mouth is large, in order to accommodate prominent upper front teeth, with the upper lip not always meeting the bottom lip due to the size of the two front teeth.

To crystallise this image, sometimes when first meeting this type you may get the impression you are looking into a horse's mouth. To match the first impression, this type can eat like a horse. In early years they do not gain much weight as they tend to exercise regularly, but in later years their weight can increase steadily.

When pure, Jupiterians are positive, confident and make good leaders. They are ambitious and others often encourage them into positions of power and responsibility, partly because of their honest and forthright nature.

These people mature early, both physically and mentally, and enjoy life's challenges, whether they be in sports, business, academia or the church. It is not uncommon for Jupiterians to reach puberty at eight or nine years of age.

Jupiterians have a strong sense of justice and fairness in all things, along with a pride in themselves and what they do. When I was working in a psychic reading shop, Boris, a Jupiterian, organised a fair system that enabled each one of us to give a reading and earn a little money. Some days were so quiet in the shop that not one customer came through the door.

As we were only paid a percentage of the money we earned, we had some lean weeks. Often we were so engrossed in conversation that we did not notice time slipping away. Boris was a great one for observing coincidence. He noticed that when one of us took a ten minute walk to stretch his or her legs or to grab a bite to eat, often the person who remained in the shop would receive some inquiries and often give a reading. He then suggested that we each leave the shop in turn, for at least half an hour, to enable the other person to earn some money. It worked.

Jupiterians' pride, and their positive open nature, suits them for a career on the stage, and they can revel in attention when it suits them. Religion, philosophy, honour, and a love of the outdoors and nature are things Jupiterians have in common. They enjoy sports, horse riding and competition, and have a slapstick sense of humour.

When trying to hang a large sign on the outside our new healing centre one afternoon, we were having a difficult time. Robert decided to climb on to the verandah roof to secure the rope. There was a resounding crash as he fell through the old corrugated iron sheets and onto some deck chairs below. I burst into the upstairs room in time to find Felix (a Jupiterian) falling over backwards from laughing so hard. Tears streamed down his face as he choked on the words: 'His . . . his face . . . the look . . . It was a classic.' From below we heard Robert's voice. 'It's okay, guys. No . . . really

. . . I can help myself up. Thanks.' Robert was not impressed.

The excess energy Jupitarians possess can make them clumsy at times, either physically or verbally, and their laughter at inappropriate moments is to cover their nervousness. They prefer honesty over tactfulness and favour the colour blue, which has a calming effect on them, balancing their occasional clumsy tendencies.

A conversation I overheard between a Jupiterian and a Venusian illustrates this verbal clumsiness.

Venusian: 'I hear that you're looking for a new place to live?'
Jupiterian: 'That's right. I've been looking for a few weeks now.'
Venusian: 'What area are you looking to move to?'
Jupiterian: 'Well, because I'm very short of money, I'm limited to looking in your neighbourhood.'

Jupiterians need a goal to reach for, a worthwhile purpose. They are lucky, as they believe in luck. Their positive attitude to life, combined with a strong desire to learn and experience the new, helps them recognise an opportunity when they see one and, through effort, turn it into a desired goal. They are not afraid to do what is necessary to achieve a goal and often seem to have great personal power. They are often aware of the influence they exert over others and this can make them vain. They are, however, warm-hearted, generous and sometimes extravagant.

Jupiterians usually resent miserliness and have a deeply religious or philosophical nature. They relate well to people from all walks of life; even when in high office, they will insist on helping the average person. This can make the Jupiterian a hero of the man in the street. Their honest, open nature means they are often favourites in the community, and people will encourage Jupiterians to take up positions of responsibility and power. Their friends and associates are usually happy to see them succeed.

Relationships

Jupiterians partner well with Apollonians and Venusians as they are all positive types. A match with a Saturnian or Lunarian could dampen the Jupiterian's enthusiasm. Being active, positive types, Jupiterians require a partner capable of keeping up with them and sharing their enthusiasm and love of the outdoors. The Martian is another good match even if the partnership becomes a little fiery at times.

Jupiterians require plenty of freedom and space in a relationship, and can sometimes enjoy the thrill of the chase more than the rewards of the partnership. This type needs to have a goal or a clear purpose to work towards, for without this, they can become restless.

Being easygoing, Jupiterians usually keep their friends. As they mature early, they tend to marry young, and to a partner of whom they can be proud. Second marriages are common, for if they marry in haste or if their partners do not cope well with the

changes in circumstances that result when Jupiterians achieve their ambitions, their first marriages tend to fail.

Careers

Jupiterians often make excellent teachers as they have the ability to take complicated examples and simplify them. They can be found teaching at schools, universities, TAFE colleges, sporting venues and so on. This teaching ability is highlighted if a 'teacher's square' appears on the Mount of Jupiter (see page 59, Figure 22).

In the early 1980s, Boris, my co-worker at the psychic shop, offered to teach me the tarot. I declined the offer because I believed that there were too many possible meanings for each tarot card, and so it would be very easy to make mistakes or to be inaccurate.

'Do you like stories?' he asked me.

'I love them. If you have a story to tell, I'm all ears.'

He then set about telling me 78 stories over the next four months, one for each tarot card. He showed me the card of the day and told me the story.

'I'm not teaching you the tarot. I'm simply telling you some stories,' he explained.

When he had told me the stories of each of the cards, he asked me to tell him a story, using seven cards which he would select at random. My task was to link all seven cards together and tell him a story. I did this and he smiled.

'That's good,' he said. 'Now can you tell

me another story using another seven cards, only this time I want you to tell me a story about travel.' I talked for half an hour about past, present and future travels and he smiled again.

'You'll make a good tarot reader.'

'But I'm not a tarot reader.'

'You are now. What do you think you were doing when you told me about my past and future travels?'

'I was only telling a story.'

'Yes, you were, yet your story accurately described what I have done in the past and most of what I plan to do in the coming months.'

He had taught me the tarot by simplifying it, by presenting it in a way I found easy to understand. Boris's 'teacher's square' gave him the ability to teach by simplifying things, without losing the basic concept.

Any career which involves leadership, achieving goals, challenges and organising others is also suitable for Jupiterians. Because of their positive and forthright nature, they are often encouraged on to further success by co-workers and management alike.

Working with horses can appeal to them, as can politics, but politics only appeals if they feel they can actually change things for the better.

Health

The Jupiterians are prone to gout, varicose veins and problems with the hips and thighs. They can be accident prone, resulting in scars and bruises, and this tendency is increased as they are sports lovers. A strong Mount of Jupiter with a full Mount of Venus and full pads at the base of the fingers confirms a great love of food. Problems with the digestive system can result if they gain weight. Generally Jupiterians bounce back quickly from ill health.

The negative Jupiterian

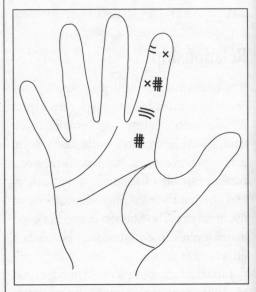

Figure 23 *Lines and signs detailing the negative Jupiterian*

The negative Jupiterian is recognised by a grille on the mount, a twisted or crooked first finger, or a series of dots or crosses on the mount.

Negative Jupiterians tend to be overweight, clumsy, raucous and vain. The men go bald early and they have loud, grating voices. They can be miserly, overbearing, greedy and completely tactless. They are intemperate and changeable with regard to their affections and responsibilities. They are ambitious for power but irresponsible using it.

I was driving through the snow-covered mountains with a typical negative Jupiterian some years ago. He was in a hurry and the car slid off the icy road into a tree as he tried to negotiate a curve. No great damage was done, so he drove off again at the same speed. We skidded off the road again at the next curve and hit another tree. Still the car suffered only panel damage, so again we sped off down the mountain. It was only after we hit a third tree and I shouted at him that he actually slowed down.

Negative Jupiterians are impatient, restless and undisciplined; very much like wild horses. They can suffer from indigestion, as they tend to eat quickly and don't know when to stop.

It is wise to lock away precious china when these people are around, for you can be sure they will break it, given half a chance. The following example illustrates the type.

The banquet hall was filled to capacity for an elaborate black tie dinner, and I sat at a table of 12 guests, opposite a couple who looked as though they always ate in such salubrious surrounds. During dessert I was distracted from a conversation with my partner by a nudge from the negative Jupiterian next to me. He was hiding his face behind his hands, as he couldn't control his laughter. He gestured to the woman opposite, so I looked over. She was immaculate. The string of pearls and the

soft green silk dress were faultless. She sat composed as she listened to the older man sitting next to her.

Then I noticed her hair. Swept into a bun atop her head, in a simple yet elegant style, was her blonde hair, and protruding from the top of the bun was a fork. Yes, the Jupiterian alongside me had managed to fling his fork across the table and into her hair!

'It just jumped out of my hand,' he insisted between fits of laughter.

To see this negative type in action you need only see the movie *The Party*, starring Peter Sellers. As an unwanted but mistakenly invited guest, he single-handedly ruins a society party, an enormous house and a couple of relationships, not to mention the odd career and the sleep of two young children and their nanny.

One negative Jupiterian I know, when mowing the lawn, managed to cut through his shoes and mow off the tips of his toes off in his haste. Another would not so much park his car as abandon it, four feet from the curb with the windows down and a door open, and there it would stand for hours at a time. With typical Jupiterian luck, the car was never stolen, even though the keys were often left in the ignition.

Negative Jupiterians are selfish, as are all the other spoiled types. They tend to embark on a project with no clear idea of how to complete it. They can lack commitment in relationships or, if married, seek other partners, preferring freedom to stability. 'More is better' can be the general attitude of this type.

THE MOUNT OF SATURN

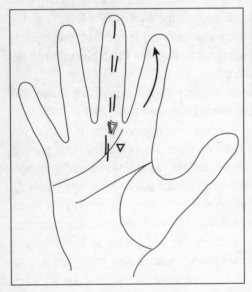

Figure 24 *Lines and signs on the Mount of Saturn*

The Mount of Saturn will rarely be full and fleshy, but one or more vertical lines or a grille can increase its strength. In pure Saturnians, the apex of the mount is found in the centre of the mount, and the apexes of surrounding mounts lean towards Saturn. The Saturn finger stands upright and the surrounding fingers lean towards it, as though for strength. A square on the mount can also increase its strength.

Saturnians are the tallest of all the types, and are thin, bony and serious in appearance and nature. They have pale, yellow skin, which is rough, dry, wrinkled and sometimes scaly (dry and flaking). The pure types are bilious, hence the skin is yellow. The face is thin, long and often pointed or bony, and the men often lose their hair prematurely. The cheeks are sunken, the eyebrows thick — in the men they tend to grow over the nose, which is long, straight and thin. Charles Dickens' character Scrooge is a classic Saturnian.

Saturnians' eyes are deep set and usually sparkle or glisten when they are angry or suspicious. The whites of the eyes are often yellow in colour. The mouth is large, with thin, pale lips and teeth which decay early in life. The gums are pale and the teeth are often yellow. The chin is prominent and, if the neck is long, this type is easily recognised by a large Adam's apple.

The men are thin-chested, the women masculine in build and nature. The body appears thin and undernourished, and blood circulation is poor.

Saturnians are not usually enthusiastic people and their bodies bear this out. They are not built for sport, fun or physical pursuits. They tend to be cynical and sceptical, and are often prudent, wise and cautious. 'Better the devil you know than the devil you don't' is one Saturnian belief; 'If you want it done properly, you'd better do it yourself' is another. They can sometimes be gloomy, unsociable and lacking in enthusiasm. They can see no point in parties, leisure or social gatherings, and instead prefer to work hard and save money. They achieve their greatest success in later life, and actor/director Clint Eastwood is typical of the build and type, although he appears more positive than is usual with Saturnians.

Saturnians often prefer the country life to that of the city, because of the space and privacy it offers, and are much more at home with plants and animals than with people. They have a talent for locating wells, underground water, oil or minerals as they have an affinity with the earth.

Saturnians are students. While others may prefer company, they prefer books. They can labour through the most tedious and uninspiring literature in their quest for knowledge, and they finish what they begin.

I recently read for a pure type who demonstrated the Saturnian's balanced approach to duty and responsibility. He was a man in his seventies who had separated from his wife so that he could devote his last remaining years to his spiritual needs and to spiritual discipline. He explained further: 'I have no television and I don't read the newspapers. My goal is to remain in this world while not being bogged down by it. I love to take long walks and I'm a keen gardener. These things keep me grounded, connected to the real world, and I have no need for the fleeting images and distractions the media offers me.'

This Saturnian had discharged his duty to his family and his career, and was fulfilling his duty to his soul and to himself. When I had completed the reading, he scoured my bookcase for anything he might want to read. He has plenty of time to read now and he is making the most of it. Subjects which interest Saturnians include agriculture, mathematics, chemistry, physics, quantum physics and quantum mechanics.

Saturnians are suspicious of the motives of others, often wary of being cheated. This is partly due to their own way of thinking, which itself is not always honest or straightforward. They often think of ways to outwit and take advantage of others, with the rationale that 'I'm only making up for all the time/money/opportunities I've lost.'

In business, they prefer to be in control, as they resent being told what to do. They are better off working for themselves or without supervision. Partnerships are not often favoured as they lack trust in others. Any business partnership does not usually last very long in any case, as the Saturnian seeks opportunities to gain complete control.

Saturnians conceal their material worth, preferring to wear old clothes, and constantly complain about how poorly they are doing. An example of this is a man I know, who worked 60–80 hours a week almost all his working life. In his late sixties, having retired, he was hospitalised and underwent heart bypass surgery. Realising that his life might soon be over, he began to spend some of his money. Within six months he built a country home, bought a large Mercedes Benz, a speed boat and a few more things he had always wanted. When this quiet, impecunious looking man died, he turned out to be a millionaire ten times over.

Saturnians can be slow to start things, but are steady and tenacious. Most of them are hard working and their success usually comes from their own efforts. They are not the type to rely on favours from friends or associates. 'A little hard work is good for you' is the attitude held by many Saturnians. I learned as a child that it was dangerous to say I was bored, for my Saturnian mother would counter with 'Oh, you're bored are you? Well, I've just the job for you. Too much time on your hands eh? A little hard work will soon cure your boredom. Here. Do this. And when you've finished let me know, for I'll have something else for you to do.' It only took a day or two of unending chores to realise that for some people, peace only comes at the end of the work, or at the end of their lives, whichever comes first.

The pure type instinctively knows that they are not attractive to others and settles into a solitary life. It could be that others have so restricted them that they prefer their own company. Often they cannot truly be themselves until they are by themselves. They worry about their reputations and tend to be conservative. They sometimes entertain wild thoughts about fighting for complete liberty, but usually do not care to risk their reputation to act upon these thoughts.

Saturnians adjust to change slowly, prefer to be in control of situations which involve them, and tend towards dark colours in clothing and furniture, including greys, browns and black. They do not feel the need to keep up with fashion and sometimes consider it a waste of money.

Saturnians often love classical, structured music and tend towards melancholy works. They prefer paintings of nature, including forests, fields and animals, to those of people.

It is unlikely that you would ever read for a pure type, for they do not usually spend the money on a reading when they could buy or borrow a book on the subject and study it for themselves. In the few cases where I have read for pure Saturnians, they have invariably produced a detailed list of questions, gone well over the allotted time (to ensure value for money) and then complained that it was all inaccurate (as a means for obtaining a complete refund of their money).

Saturnians often do not relate well to children because they were not children themselves when they were young. This type starts life as an old person, and begins to grow younger at around 58–60 years of age. If they live into their eighties, Saturnians can become quite eccentric, careless of reputation and lively.

A strong Mount of Saturn can describe someone who had a father or father figure who was either very strict and old-fashioned or who was never present, physically or emotionally, during the child's early years. In some cases, the father may have died or left the home before the person's 14th birthday. This can mean that he or she had to take on responsibility at an early age, which can lead to the belief that life is harsh and unforgiving.

Women with a prominent Mount of Saturn can display a contempt for men, preferring the company of women. Alternately, they can find themselves attracted to older men, or to men who appear strong, stable and financially secure yet turn out to be weak and rigid. This type of experience can leave the Saturnian woman with a mild contempt for men, as beliefs have a way of proving themselves. Many homosexual women have strong Mounts of Saturn or other signs which strengthen this mount.

Saturnian women achieve a great deal in career and material terms. They may forego having a family in favour of a career, but if they do have children they tend to keep working rather than stay at home, for they treasure financial independence. I have seen Saturnian women marry men who take on the role of 'house husband', raising the children and perhaps working from home.

One couple, a Saturnian woman and a Lunarian man, have a comfortable arrangement. She is a police detective and he is a writer. She has recently given birth to their child, which he looks after at home while she goes to work. If it meant raising the child herself, at home, she probably would not have considered a family. He is a homebody, and realises that she can earn twice what he could, so both of them are happy.

Relationships

Saturnians are solitary by nature, and in the pure form do not usually contemplate marriage. Why marry and support someone when your money and effort can be put to better use? They do not need the company of others, so usually marry for money, security or to have someone look after their needs: to cook, clean and so on. They tend to partner with Lunarians, for neither are passionate types.

They can be controlling and aloof, needing a great deal of physical and emotional space. They usually have a room or a part of the house which is exclusively theirs for privacy.

When pure Saturnians do marry and have children, they can be a tyrannical parents, being both restrictive and old-fashioned. However, they mellow with age, becoming quite tolerant and even somewhat open-minded in their sixties and seventies. This can make Saturnians better grandparents than parents.

Careers

Saturnians are the hardest working of all the types, but this in itself does not guarantee their success. They prefer to do everything themselves, as they believe other people are unreliable.

Saturnians are suited to careers in chemistry, mathematics, physics, geology, engineering and farming. Those with coarse hands (hands with hard, dry skin and only the main lines on the palms) can sometimes turn their interest in chemicals to manufacturing drugs; for instance, distilling heroin from morphine or working in a chemical production factory. Those with fine hands (hands with soft skin and many fine lines accompanying the main lines) can be found working in pharmaceuticals, researching herbal medicines or writing scientific books or journals.

Saturnians can also do well with real estate, accountancy, banking, politics, philosophy and the Church (often in a sect where suffering and deprivation are required of the followers). They are often found in the police force and in courts of law. They may be judges, legal counsel, police detectives or defendants. Their propensity for study suits them to the law, particularly for the responsibilities involved in deciding the fate of others, as a judge might do regularly.

They can also be writers, especially of non-fiction. Politics, science, history, economics, agriculture and the occult are subjects which they write about successfully for, although scientific and sceptical, they can also be superstitious.

Health

Saturnians often have liver problems, which causes excess bile to find its way into the digestive system and then the blood. Once in the blood, bile is a poison, and the blood deposits it in the skin. Hence the skin is yellow, the colour of bile.

If you have ever suffered with food poisoning, you probably remember how quickly you lost your sense of humour and positive outlook. This might help you to understand Saturnians, who seem to suffer a permanent mild poisoning which accounts for their rather bleak outlook on life.

Saturnians suffer from nervous problems, which affect the knees and legs, occasionally resulting in paralysis below the waist. Tooth decay and skin allergies are also common, as is trouble with the ears.

Hands which have a blue tinge indicate susceptibility to haemorrhoids and varicose veins. Fluted, brittle nails suggest the onset of nervous disease, which may lead to complications in later life. Sloped shoulders tend to close in on the chest and lungs, giving this type little oxygen for life and therefore little liveliness.

The negative Saturnian

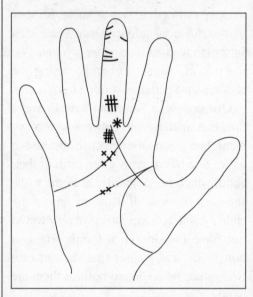

Figure 25 *Lines and signs detailing the negative Saturnian*

An excessively grilled mount, a broken or chained Line of Heart, a crooked Saturn finger and a hard hand are indicators of a negative type. When negative, Saturnians can have stooped shoulders, a hunched back, crossed eyes, scant hair and/or leathery skin. They can be pessimistic, and have a tendency to commit suicide if gloom hovers for too long over their lives.

Negative Saturnians are often stingy and go to unbelievable lengths to avoid spending money. I shared a house with a negative Saturnian man some years back, and I would come home in the evening to find one solitary candle burning. It was not that he preferred the romantic, soft glow of the candlelight, or that the power was off, but that he believed it to be cheaper to run a candle than an electric light bulb.

He kept all his money under his mattress, convinced that banks were only a way of other people knowing how much money you have. Having soft hands, he preferred not to work, and was a collector of anything he hoped might have worth. When he moved out of his previous rented premises, he took with him a few things he felt entitled to after paying 'so much rent all those years', including the stove, the fireplace and mantle, the power points and globes.

Even though he'd cleaned the landlord out, he still felt cheated. I tried to explain to him that the signing of a residential lease was an agreement to pay money periodically for the use of the premises, but he argued that by being there he was actually doing the landlord a favour, as he prevented squatters from moving in.

Negative Saturnians usually do not trust anyone, believing that others think in the same deviant way they do. This is a criminal type, from computer or white-collar crime through to petty theft. Their rationale tends to be along the lines of 'Those rich people can afford it after ripping us off all those years'. Only their intense fear of imprisonment or restriction (lack of privilege) holds their criminal tendencies in check. They prefer poisoning as their first choice if planning a murder.

Some years ago I saw a woman being interviewed on television; she was being questioned about the death of each of her three husbands from what was believed to have been poisoning. She denied the accusations, but her crossed eyes, pointed nose and Saturnian features left me wondering about her innocence.

As criminals they tend to be repeat offenders. Whereas pure Saturnians work long and hard for what they want, the negative type often looks for a 'short cut'. Any time they spend in prison is merely time to lay down a better plan. This is the very reason why Saturnians make good detectives — they think like their opponents.

THE MOUNT OF SUN/APOLLO

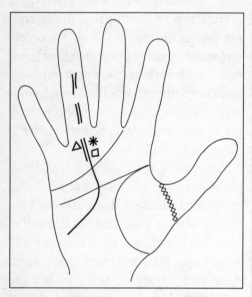

Figure 26 *Lines and signs on the Mount of Sun/Apollo (note the long Apollo finger)*

Apollonians can be recognised by a long, independent Apollo finger and by a Line of Sun/Apollo. A star, triangle, circle, single vertical line or square strengthen this mount. However, many vertical lines tend to dissipate the energy of this mount.

A long Apollo finger will often be longer than the Jupiter finger. Its normal length is half way up the first phalange of the Saturn finger. If it is longer than this, and not due to a shorter-than-average Saturn finger, then the Apollo qualities are increased.

Apollonians are usually of medium height, and of a build in between that of the Jupiterian and the Saturnian. In other words, they are neither fleshy nor lean and lanky, but shapely, muscular and athletic, with curvaceous body lines. A broad, low forehead and large almond-shaped eyes with long lashes which curl up at the ends are traits of this type.

The eyes change as emotion comes into play, and they betray a quick mind and a sympathetic nature. The cheeks are firm and rounded, not hollow. The neck is long, not fleshy and does not have a large Adam's apple. The voice is musical but not resonant, giving it a softer quality than that of the other types.

Apollonians have a spring in their step, due to the finely balanced body and mind, and a natural aptitude for sports, gymnastics and dancing. Apollonians are usually healthy, vigorous, enthusiastic and attractive to others. Other types often find them confident and positive, hence they are popular. They are spontaneous, versatile, love beauty and can be very creative.

Apollonians are very aware of harmony and disharmony around them, in words, people, furnishings, colours, fabrics, clothes and so on. They can sometimes experience difficulty relating to people whom they feel are not attractive, because of the great value they place on beauty. They love fine clothes, luxurious home furnishings, lavish entertaining and jewels. With a long first phalange, they display subtlety in combining these things, but when the third phalange is longest or very full, they can be loud, showy and lacking in a sense of style.

More than any other type, Apollonians need to express themselves, whether through writing, talking, painting, acting or sport. Very playful by nature, they can exhibit a gentle, teasing sense of humour.

This is a very artistic mount, but often it shows an appreciation of the beautiful rather than the ability to produce beautiful things. However, if an Apollonian has a long first phalange or the apex of the mount is in the centre, it indicates creative talent.

To the Apollonian, it is enough that a thing be beautiful. It need not function, be practical or be economically or morally balanced. Oscar Wilde, an Apollonian, demonstrates the sense of humour by putting it this way: 'We can forgive a man for making a useful thing as long as he does not admire it. The only excuse for making a useless thing is that one admires it intensely. All art is quite useless.'

Apollonians can be successful in business because of their versatility and creative approach to all things. These people naturally attract creative opportunities, wealth and fame. They are highly intuitive and learn as though remembering rather than through laborious means. This is especially so for art and literature. Apollonians do not work as hard to learn as Saturnians and can therefore lack the depth of Saturnians.

Apollonians have the ability to make a brilliant display of their knowledge, even when it is limited. They do this by expanding on an idea once they have grasped it, often getting credit for ideas and theories they didn't come up with. They can leave you believing that they know a great deal about a topic, for they know when to change the subject.

These people are inventive, especially if they have spatulate fingernails, and are natural mimics. This can make them successful in the fields of acting, sales, motivation and communication.

Apollonians speak with intuition and often learn without study. As teachers, they can make any subject interesting, humorous and attractive to students. One Apollonian, when learning the names of psychological disorders and of the drugs used to treat them, put the whole list to music and made them the new words to a favourite song. He played the song regularly on the piano, enjoying the game of learning. In the exam, he was the only student humming away quietly to himself.

Apollonians are often the centre of attention and can adapt themselves to any situation. Possessing brilliant and adaptable minds, they feel at home with any group of people and can always find something in common with anyone they meet.

This type is often a public favourite, and whereas Saturnians tend to shun publicity, Apollonians love it, and in turn the public enjoys helping them to achieve their goals. Actors, film stars, media personalities, singers, painters and dancers usually have strong Mount of Apollo.

Because of their brilliance, Apollonians sometimes find that those who envy them become their enemies. This type enjoys success, which seems to come naturally, and they are rarely very good at holding onto money, as they spend what they have and believe that the future will take care of itself. They usually make their money in short bursts of brilliant achievement, and others often gladly help them on to greater success.

Apollonians are usually gifted with strong intuition and are interested in the occult, though they do not usually study it as deeply as Saturnians or Plutonians. They tend to be cheerful, happy, bright and have a balanced temper. When angry they can lash out, but they quickly get over it and usually hold no resentment.

Being changeable, they tend not to develop deep and lasting friendships. Apollonians will often go far in search of beautiful scenery, well-executed art and good conversation. They are usually law abiding, knowing that they don't need to steal for they can easily earn enough money to buy what they require.

These people frequently retain much of a child's spontaneous sense of fun, enjoying what they do in life and intuitively picking things that they will be successful in. The longer the Apollo finger, the more chances the person will take in life and the more the artistic tendencies rule.

When the lower part of the hand and third phalanges of the fingers are the most developed, it indicates physical creativity. Gymnastics, dancing, pottery, food, clothing, jewellery and sculpture are just some of the possibilities. When the middle (or social) part of the hand and the second phalanges of the fingers are the most developed, it indicates a talent for business, entertainment and communication. When the upper phalanges of the fingers are full and the fingers are the most developed part of the hand, it shows a gift for poetry, painting, writing and an artistic life.

Smooth fingers are natural to Apollonians, being an impulsive, intuitive type, and knotty fingers interfere with the Apollonian's intuition and spontaneity, which are the main sources of strength in this type.

Relationships

Apollonians can be unhappy in marriage. The search for someone who shines as brightly as they like to is a hard one, and they often settle for a partner who would love to shine but does not 'have what it takes'. This means they have to be content merely to dream of the life they want, unless they divorce and try again.

They can also experience difficulties with ego boundaries when in a relationship. The symptoms of this can be that they focus solely on their partner and the relationship at the cost of friends, career and hobbies. Should problems occur within the relationship, Apollonians may turn their attention to their career, with great results but at the cost of the relationship. It is a little like a see-saw, with career at one end and a relationship at the other.

Apollonians can be in love with the idea of love. The day-to-day reality of living with someone becomes a chain around their necks if they cannot be romantic and express their love in inspired ways.

Apollonians match well with Jupiterians or Venusians. They are not as ambitious in marriage as Jupiterians can be, and prefer someone for whom they can shine. Lunarians and the Neptunians can be attracted to Apollonians because of their ability to make everyday things larger than life, but these types are often mismatched. Lunarians and Neptunians can slow an Apollonian down and, in time, the Apollonian will become hard or even bitter at missing life's opportunities by being 'out of step' with his or her own life.

The Martian type often becomes a little impatient with the Apollonian, while the Saturnian can find the Apollonian too social and careless with money. The Apollonian matches well with fellow Apollonians and sometimes with Mercurians.

With spatulate fingertips and nails, Apollonians can have a little more in common with Martians. The second most prominent mount in the hands will give more detail as to an appropriate partner; for instance, an Apollonian with a Saturn secondary mount is likely to get along well with a Saturnian, particularly if the Saturnian has a well-developed Mount of Apollo.

Careers

Apollonians often choose a career that will put them in the public eye. Acting, singing (indicated by a full Mount of Venus), painting and sculpting appeal to this type. They can also be found in jobs which involve selling, communication and motivation.

No matter what their job, Apollonians work with flair, adding their personal stamp to the task at hand, and approach their career with enthusiasm and a sense of fun.

Routine work is unsuitable for Apollonians, and if faced with a restricted routine they will change jobs regularly. Noel is a perfect example of the type. His first choice of career was acting, but, unable to make a living from acting, he took up a position as an accounts clerk in a large company. Within five months he was frustrated and restless with the day-to-day routine. Desperately unhappy, he wanted to leave, but could not find another job. Through the months that followed, he began to lose interest in going to work, and often arrived late, took long lunch breaks and left early. One afternoon, after arriving two hours late that morning and having taken a two-hour lunch break, his supervisor called him aside to admonish him for his lateness. It was then that Noel resigned and resumed his acting career.

Health

Generally Apollonians are healthy, and their athletic nature and love of life helps they to stay in that way. Their food intake is not as excessive as a Jupiterian's and they prefer variety and novelty in what they eat.

The heart is a common problem area for

Apollonians and blue nails confirm heart trouble. They often have problems with their eyesight, and an island on the Line of Heart under Apollo can signify heart or eyesight trouble. Check the rest of the hand for confirmation. Cross bars on the mount confirm heart trouble, and a small dot on the Line of Health under Apollo indicates eye trouble.

Occasional fevers and back trouble can also be found with this type. Bulbous nails can signify lung trouble, but this is rare.

The negative Apollonian

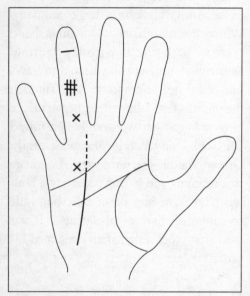

Figure 27 *Lines and signs detailing the negative Apollonian*

A thick third phalange and a short first phalange, or a crooked Apollo finger with short nails, indicates a negative Apollonian. Hard hands, with no flexibility at the fingers, a chained Line of Heart or a large cross on the mount can also increase the negative Apollo tendencies. Four or five of the above signs must be found to safely suggest a negative type.

Negative Apollonians are usually vain, arrogant and competitive, and routinely want the lion's share of attention, praise, recognition and material rewards. They love to boast and can display an inflated opinion of themselves. They crave notoriety, going to great lengths to make themselves conspicuous. They can betray their principles in their quest for fame.

Negative Apollonians are the type who will interrupt someone mid-sentence with something they feel it is more important to discuss. They talk but do not listen. They crave an audience and need to be idolised, resorting to being the hero in front of small children if need be. They can display the 'I, the King' syndrome — they think they are better than everyone else. This gives spoiled Apollonians licence to spend hours boasting about their achievements or to criticise those who have genuine success.

They long to be leaders but, without self-discipline or any good nature to speak of, they rarely achieve such heights. This can make them bitter and vengeful, or contemptuous of those who have success in their chosen field.

The negative type can gamble all their money away and then seek to gamble yours as well, if you allow them. They live today on the money they hope to earn tomorrow. Even when poor, they spend extravagantly on clothes and things which they feel improve their image. However, they seldom turn to crime to satisfy these urges.

Josh is a typical negative Apollonian. He is always penniless, but drives a Jaguar and usually manages to wear a clean, pressed suit to the endless lunches he juggles on various credit cards. Negative Apollonians are very image conscious and can be shallow; they can give Saturnians good reason to shun people and hide away in books.

Negative Apollonians with soft hands are completely lazy, starting much and finishing little. They feel as though someone should 'sponsor' them, and that life owes them a living. They wonder why the world has not realised how talented they really are. These 'would be' writers or painters spend years at a time with 'writer's block' while their partners support them.

These people can be magnets for fights and disagreements, and the women enjoy the physical discharge that accompanies a loud and passionate argument. Negative Apollonians tease people mercilessly, given half a chance, and they have a complete lack of compassion for others. Their small mouths and thin lips can make them recognisable at a distance.

These people are often unhappy, and compete with all who would be their friends. They tend to suffer from heart trouble (angina or an irregular heartbeat) in their later years, along with muscle spasms and poor eyesight. They are often 'hard-hearted', which can be due to pain and hardship, or because they were rejected or ignored early on in life. However, if they feel needed and useful, and that they do belong in an equal sense to a group, they can overcome some of this hardness.

THE MOUNT OF MERCURY

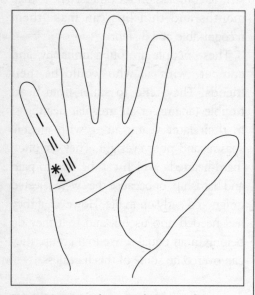

Figure 28 *Lines and signs on the Mount of Mercury*

When the Mercury finger is independent, straight and strong, and the apex is centrally located with a full Mount of Mercury, the person is a Mercurian. When a star, triangle, circle, single vertical line or square are present on the mount, the Mercurian qualities are increased.

Mercurians are usually small, with an oval face and smooth, fine skin which often looks youthful. They are neat and tidy in appearance. The eyes are small, close-set, sharp and restless, often analysing, observing and judging. The nose is thin, straight and somewhat fleshy on the end. Thin lips and slightly yellow whites of the

eyes are usual with this type. The teeth are white, small and even.

They tend to be of a nervous disposition and are usually active, both mentally and physically. They are quick in movement and their bodies are flexible. They often run on nervous energy and can become drained from time to time. Regular rest and spending time outdoors helps restore this nervous energy. Regular meditation can also help.

Mercurians enjoy sports and games of skill, often winning because they plan their moves and shrewdly size up their opponents. They are good judges of character and possess crystal clear memories. Names, dates and numbers are quickly recalled, and facts that most of us would not bother to remember, Mercurians store away for later use.

Mercurians often have the advantage in an argument, as they are quick of mind and tongue. They can grasp a point and turn the whole argument around before you have realised what has happened. This makes the Mercurian a natural communicator or salesperson, saying the right thing at the right time to close the sale.

They are able to judge others quickly by observation and analysis, and by recalling similar types of people. They are constantly scheming and planning, but give little indication as to what they are planning, for although they love to question others, they can be very closed when others probe into their natures.

Mercurians are clever managers, and can organise people and situations with a minimum of fuss and still manage to stay in the background. This type understands humanity clearly and uses this knowledge to their advantage.

Peter is Mercurian and his partner is Martian. Janet will pick a fight in a typical Martian fashion and Peter will try to avoid confrontation. When he tires of avoiding Janet's verbal challenges, he paints her into a corner with his clear memory of the facts and cold, hard logic. He uses his mind like a sword, deftly slicing through Janet's argument and winning a few extra concessions for himself at the same time.

Mercurians are rarely lazy unless a strong secondary mount is found, such as Venus or Luna, or the hand is very soft, though soft hands are uncommon with Mercurians. They will be working in their minds even when they appear to be resting. They love to study, especially subjects such as science, medicine, mathematics, business, accountancy and the psychic sciences, and love reading, particularly scientific and factual books. They crave information. To them, television is for news, documentaries, travel, science and technology programs. Newspapers and magazines are also important sources of information.

There is always money to be made for Mercurians. If they cannot buy some–thing to resell at a profit, they seek ways to charge money for their time (consultancy work), ideas, space and so on. Mercurians can usually sense an opportunity before anyone else and are constantly thinking of new ways to make money. They are attracted to the most profitable areas of business, including jewellery, real estate, the motion picture industry, clothing manufacture and any business where there is a high mark-up or profit margin. Years ago I mentioned to a Mercurian friend that I was studying to be a counsellor. She nodded wisely, then drily stated, 'It's as good as any other career really. One man's problem is another man's beach house, I suppose.'

Mercurians possess shrewdness, tact, diplomacy, management skills, the ability to influence others, good judgement and a great ability to express themselves, and these in combination mean Mercurians rarely fail in business. If a pure Mercurian type fails in business, sometimes it is to avoid paying tax or some other looming debt. It would probably be carefully planned.

A Mercurian friend accepted a job as a door person at a night club and resigned after the first night, as she believed that the pay was too low. She enjoyed herself throughout the seven-hour shift, as she met every person coming through the door. The word from the management was 'Don't accept her resignation. She's the best person we've had on the door in five years.'

'Didn't you talk yourself hoarse?' I asked her.

'No. I managed to catch up with a lot of people I hadn't seen in ages. Besides, it was really only one long conversation. It started around 9.30 pm and finished when the taxi driver said goodnight at about 5.30 in the morning. I could write a book about some of the things I heard that first night.'

Over the next two weeks there were many inquiries from club patrons as to her whereabouts and she eventually accepted the position again, with a sizeable increase in salary.

Mercurians also enjoy animals and nature, which calm them down a little. They typically love children, are devoted to their families and are loyal and constant in friendship. An example of the pure type is Ross Perot, the candidate for the US presidency in 1992. He cited as his reason for withdrawing from the presidential race the fact that the press put his family under constant scrutiny. He stated that he wanted to protect the privacy of his family. His attitude, his business ability and his height and shape all fit the Mercurian type.

Relationships

Mercurians frequently marry young and often choose their own type. They are often proud of their partner and enjoy seeing him or her well dressed and neatly presented. They are not stingy with money, nor extravagant like Apollonians, but invest well and usually live comfortably. Compared with the other types, the Mercurian is a moderate person.

Mercurians usually only partner well with other Mercurians, as the other types can find them too industrious and quick of pace. The second most prominent mount on the subject's hand will indicate another type who may suit; for instance, a secondary Mount of Pluto would indicate that the subject would partner well with a Plutonian.

Careers

Mercurians succeed in many walks of life due to the ease with which they communicate. They are natural organisers and can manage people effectively while remaining in the background. Unlike Apollonians, who need recognition, Mercurians prefer financial rewards, or the peace that comes from knowing that another project has been successfully completed without complications.

These people are traders, small business proprietors, financial advisers, actors, mime artists and writers. If you want someone to sell ice in Antarctica or matches in hell, your best chance of success would be to choose a Mercurian.

Several vertical lines on the Mount of Mercury indicate an ability for medical studies, especially if the Mercury finger is long and has a long middle phalange. These signs can also indicate an ability for studies in natural therapies — naturopathy, acupuncture, osteopathy, oriental medicine and so on. Four or five vertical lines indicate an interest in anatomy and physiology, and an ability to learn these subjects easily (see page 76, Figure 28).

Mercurians make good librarians, for their love of order and neatness is a natural part of library work. They are naturally suited to the advertising industry as they can make any product appealing and target the right group of potential customers. They also make excellent lawyers, using their mercurial mentality to see both sides of an argument, which they then sway in any direction they choose.

Health

Generally, Mercurians enjoy good health. They sometimes have ridged, brittle nails, which indicates a tendency for bouts of nervous exhaustion. Upward bending nails can also suggest nervous exhaustion which, if untreated over a prolonged period (about 20–30 years), could lead to a stroke or a nervous breakdown.

Some years ago, one of my students, who had a strong Mount of Mercury and upward bending nails, suffered a stroke before completing the course. By making changes to her lifestyle, she eventually made a full recovery.

Problems with the nerves can affect the liver, leading to an overproduction of bile. Unlike the Saturnian, when the Mercurian is treated, the liver returns to normal fairly quickly.

Mercurians can suffer from stomach trouble and chest and lung congestion. When the nervous exhaustion is deep and prolonged, it can lead to strokes, paralysis (often to the arms and hands) or even multiple sclerosis.

Three or more very small vertical lines found grouped together just above the Line of Heart between Mercury and Apollo can signify pancreas trouble (see page 142, Figure 80). When this sign appears, a continued high intake of sugars and sweetened foods can result in hypoglycaemia or diabetes. If these lines appear on both hands, this weakness in the pancreas area can be hereditary. I have observed that, on an emotional/psychological level, it can show someone who puts sweetness into the mouth instead of putting it into the heart.

The negative Mercurian

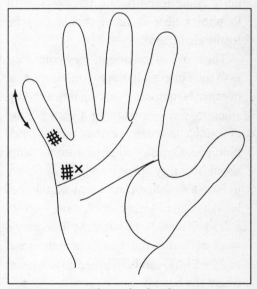

Figure 29 *Lines and signs detailing the negative Mercurian*

Negative Mercurians can be identified by a grille and/or a cross on the Mount of Mercury, a crooked Mercury finger and very stiff fingers (fingers which do not bend backwards easily). At least two of the above signs need to be present to confirm the negative qualities. Cross lines on the

Mercury finger also confirm negative tendencies.

With the pure type being so shrewd, the negative type is not too different from the original description. Negative Mercurians get a thrill from the feeling of outwitting another person, which is sometimes more rewarding than the money they may gain as a result. They are the most likely of all the types to become involved in criminal activities. Once they give in to temptation and rationalise away their guilt, it is easier to do it again. Soon they have moved from petty crime to corporate takeovers, with loopholes close at hand should they be legally challenged.

Their love of making money combined with their interest in the occult means that negative Mercurians can sometimes end up spinning yarns or painting a grim picture of your life in order to extract more money from you. Occasionally I hear from clients about how they spent hundreds of dollars to have a so-called clairvoyant rid them of bad luck, an old curse or even the spirit of a dead relative. 'Your late aunt Rosemary's spirit still haunts the house where she lived, and for $750 I can help her to go to heaven where she belongs.'

With a crooked Mercury finger, the Mercury qualities of communication are distorted. These people tend to be suspicious and often experience difficulties with love relationships, as they have trouble expressing their needs clearly. They can be dishonest with those who are close to them. This is not to say they lie constantly to their partners, but that they are unlikely to 'come clean' about who they are and what they feel and believe.

When a crooked or bent Mercury finger is found in both hands, it can indicate a person who has grown up in a family in which people avoided talking about how they were feeling. There may have been a great deal of talking, but usually to avoid or camouflage feelings.

When there is a bent Mercury finger which sits very far away from the Apollo finger, it can signify someone who has taken up a career that involves communication (e.g. sales) in order to improve his or her own ability to communicate.

Negative Mercurians with criminal tendencies can lie straight-faced while meeting your gaze, and I have heard them described as 'snake oil men' (those people who travelled America in the pioneer days selling snake oil and 'cure all' creams and ointments). Other negative Mercurians have a distinct shiftiness about them. They don't stand too long in one place and cannot face you squarely.

When there is a grille on the Mount of Mercury, a twisted Mercury finger and little or no Line of Heart, it can indicate a pickpocket, con artist, dishonest gambler, thief, counterfeiter or peddler of stolen goods, depending on the coarseness or fineness of the skin on the palm and the back of the hand (generally, the finer the texture of skin, the more refined the person's nature). Any scheme or scam that is going on will involve this type. Because they are natural mimics, forgery is particularly appealing.

Negative Mercurians with stiff hands can be stingy and old-fashioned. When the hand is yellow it increases the negative tendencies. When the nails bend away from the fingertips, the depletion of nervous energy is already apparent and the person will need to relax and meditate regularly. When the apex of the mount is towards the outside of the hand, the person can be selfishly inclined.

No matter how honest they appear to be, negative Mercurians are likely to step over the line and make more money than ever before, in not quite legal circumstances. I grew up watching my neighbour, a negative Mercurian, sell one car after another, all of them dangerous wrecks. He sold a car with the paint yet to dry, and another which had been on fire twice that morning. When he damaged a car in a small accident, he parked it in the street and rented it out as accommodation to a homeless girl. No point in having it sitting there when it could be earning him money!

THE MOUNT OF MARS

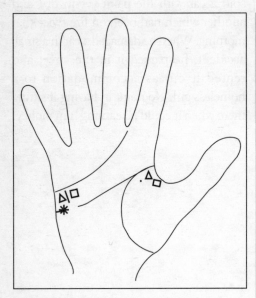

Figure 30 *Lines and signs on the Mount of Mars*

Lyndall was turning 40 and her husband Lawrie arranged a surprise party for her. We were given strict instructions not to park anywhere near the house — he wanted her to be completely surprised. Surprised is not quite the word to describe how she must have felt.

We gathered expectantly in the kitchen, holding presents, champagne and streamers and looking at the swing door which was closed in front of us. Her car pulled into the driveway and the excitement level rose as we heard the key in the front door. Lawrie looked up from his newspaper in a studied, casual manner as she came through the door. Before he could even say hello, she began.

'That's just great. I'm standing here with a truck load of groceries and all you can do is read the paper. The trouble with you Lawrie is that you're lazy. Lazy and unmotivated. I work, look after the kids, get the food and cook it. You go to work, if you could call it that, and then you come home and eat. I'm sick of it.'

We all froze. Trapped inside someone's house listening to an argument was not quite what we expected. On and on she went about how she was never going to cook again and how all she really needed was a drink. She was still loudly voicing her opinion as she pushed open the swing door to the kitchen to reveal 14 distinctly uneasy people.

Upon seeing us she screamed. It dis–pelled the tension and we knew our first word was an understatement. 'Surprise!' we chorused, and our Martian friend reached for the nearest champagne bottle with 'Somebody give me a drink'. Two hours later she was dancing wildly with Lawrie, displaying the typical Martian passion.

There are two mounts of Mars on the palm — Upper Mars and Lower Mars. **The Mount of Upper Mars** lies directly beneath the Mount of Mercury and under the Line of Heart (see page 132). It extends about two to three centimetres across from the edge of the hand (the percussion). **The Mount of Lower Mars** is the fleshy pad beneath the Mount of Jupiter and above the thumb.

A person can be described as a Martian when either one of these mounts is prominent, and when single lines, crosses, stars, triangles or squares are found on either mount. The mounts of Upper and Lower Mars are linked by the Plain of Mars, which lies between the lines of Head and Heart.

Martians are generally of strong build, medium height, with a small, strong head. They can have a wide face with strong cheekbones, large (sometimes bloodshot) eyes and a large mouth with small, yellowish teeth. The eyebrows are generally strong and low, giving Mercurians a scowl-like appearance. A Roman nose (strong and straight), a strong chin and small, close-set ears are found with this type.

Martians usually have a short, thick neck, broad shoulders and an expansive chest. If you watch a rugby or football match you will see a good selection of these people. They are brave and thrive on conflict, so they are attracted to the armed forces. They are energetic, generous, devoted and loyal to their friends, and will fight for their friends when necessary.

A young man sat down for a tarot reading recently and, as he shuffled the cards, I noticed his small head, close-set ears and the single eyebrow which grew across the bridge of his nose. I asked him if he was interested in the military or in martial arts.

'It's funny you should ask that. My first question is whether I will get into the Air Force, and if not, should I try for the Navy.'

Lower Mars represents aggression and Upper Mars represents resistance. These people are fighters. In Greek and Roman mythology, Mars or Ares was the god of War. Cross these people and you can quickly come face to face with a warrior. In most hands, a person's temper and control of such are shown by both the mounts of Mars and the Plain of Mars.

Vladimir and Rosemary have reverse mounts to one another and it shows in their temperaments. He has a full Lower Mars but no Upper Mars. She has a moderate Lower Mars and a strong Upper Mars. He will lose his temper two or three times a day, for he has little control of it, exemplified by a lack of Upper Mars. Rosemary, however, loses her temper only once or twice a year, but when she does, Vladimir doesn't forget it. She has great control of her temper (Upper Mars) but when she finally lets it loose, much that has built up rushes out. Vladimir is considered 'bad tempered' whereas he is actually undisciplined.

When the Plain of Mars is much crossed with fine lines (often red), it indicates a sudden temper. A hollow palm shows an inability to sustain an outburst of temper.

Martians with a strong Upper Mars are cool, calm in emergencies, and do not give up easily. Long after others have given in, they will be found resolutely working towards their goals. They are often successful for this very reason alone. Even those with little or no talent will enjoy some success, due to their perseverance.

Those with a well-developed Lower Mars push heartily towards their goals, seeking strife and loving it. A few scars denote a good battle won. They can be inconsiderate of others, forcing through their plans aggressively. Martians with a prominent Lower Mars love to fight for a cause. Whether it be freedom, better pay and conditions, political, environmental or military, they will be there, giving it their best shot. One Martian friend is always involved in union affairs in her workplace, and is quick to jump into the disputes of others, even contributing to an escalation of tension at times. She seems to find it hard to sit back and allow others to resolve their own differences.

Those with a full Lower Mars and a poor Upper Mars commonly bluff their way through situations, but when challenged or put under pressure are likely to give in or back down.

Martians enjoy competitive sports: boxing, wrestling, martial arts, fencing, shooting, hunting, football, motorcycle racing, motor boats and fast cars. The more blood spilled the better. This is not an intellectual or studious type, hence very fine texture of skin is not common to this type, as they tend towards a physical rather than an intellectual approach. They like to be physically involved to know that they're alive. One pure type summed it up with 'Sometimes you've got to break it to fix it.'

They are 'manly' men and strong, forceful women. A friend with a strong Upper and Lower Mars never misses an opportunity to watch live motor racing and thoroughly enjoys each Grand Prix she attends, especially the explosions, accidents and wrecked cars. She says that she finds motor racing more exciting than any other sport.

With a Line of Mars (a short line on Lower Mars which follows the Line of Life — see page 152, Figure 97), these people experience great difficulty staying out of other people's arguments. Where the Saturnian walks away and the Mercurian stands close enough to observe the action, the Martian is usually in the heart of the action within moments. If you were selecting a soldier to capture a territory it would be advantageous to send a person with a strong Lower Mars, whereas to defend a territory, a person with a strong Upper Mars would be a better choice.

Martians are well meaning, determined and often tactless. Typically they are very amorous, passionate and preoccupied with the opposite sex. When they fall in love it is usually a passionate affair: sensual, unsentimental and physical.

They love food, especially the kind that will fill them up: meat, eggs, game, poultry, potatoes and solid foods. To the Martian, salad is mere decoration. They usually enjoy rich, spicy food and red wine. They tend towards excess but, with a robust health, they tend to weather the effects quite well. It is not advisable to attempt to drink this type under the table, for you will probably lose unless you are also a Martian.

I recently spent a week on a farm, looking

after the house while the owner was away overseas. Though I hadn't met him, a quick glance around his house confirmed a Martian type. Home-dried chillies filled enormous jars, in quantities only a restaurant would need, confirming the Martian love of spicy food. The furniture was mostly leather, and anything made of cloth was various shades of red, a favourite colour of Martians. Even the token dried flower arrangement was several shades of deep red. I counted three guns, along with two motorbikes, an archery set and four horses. Perhaps he has a Jupiter secondary mount, or maybe the archery set belonged to the boy with the large front teeth in the photographs about the place. I guessed it was his son.

Martians love music with pronounced rhythms and fiery arrangements with plenty of brass instruments. Military bands generally do not include violins and cellos.

Relationships

Martians partner well with Venusians, as Martians are usually masculine and Venusians feminine. Lunarians can also be a good match, provided they don't prove too sensitive to the directness of the Mars energy. Jupiterians match well, but this relationship can become a fiery arrangement as the Jupiterian loves plenty of freedom and the Martian (who also loves freedom) can display deep jealousy and a brooding possessiveness.

Martians can be attracted to the aloofness of Saturnians and the challenge it represents, but for this to be a lasting relationship, each partner requires complementary secondary mounts; that is, Venus or Pluto. An example of the Martian type is the late actor, Richard Burton, who also possessed strong Pluto qualities.

Careers

A career in the military appeals to Martian types, as does one in the police force, the fire brigade or the ambulance service. Careers requiring a strong stomach and a sense of adventure or competition are also obvious choices for Martians: boxing, martial arts, fencing, football, motorcycle racing, motor boat and car racing.

Martians can also be found working in the construction industry or as plumbers. They can often be found working with metal or wood. Those with a strong Upper Mars have an affinity for metal, so careers such as mechanical engineering and welding are appealing. Those with a strong Lower Mars have an affinity for wood, and these people are suited to carpentry, furniture restoration and so on.

Union delegates and traders in old and new weapons are often Martians, for these people are attracted to conflict because of the excitement it provides.

Health

Martians are prone to scars caused by accidents, battles and sheer recklessness. They can suffer headaches or bumps to the head when Lower Mars is well-developed and problems with the sexual organs when Upper Mars is strong.

The colour of the skin helps determine the type of health problems likely to be experienced. Red increases sensuality and temper. Pink is a healthy balance. White is unusual in this type and it reduces strength. Yellow signifies bile, and this can make for a vicious temperament.

Bronchial difficulties can be common, and are indicated by fluted, narrow nails. Being fighters, there is a high incidence of broken bones or noses with this type. I recall a pair of hands which were completely disfigured with scars and cuts and badly set broken bones. The man, a Martian, shrugged. 'Oh, that! I used to punch parked cars when I was young. I reset the bones myself. I even did my own stitches at home, on my dad's workbench.' He saw it as being tough, and no loss, for he never intended to play the piano.

A woman recently placed her hands on my table, and I noticed the Mercury finger on her left hand would not open out naturally. 'Have you broken your little finger at some stage?' I asked her.

'No. My husband cut my tendons with a knife. He lost his temper and slashed my hand.'

Later in the reading I noticed a break in her Line of Life at around 38 years of age. 'There was a touch and go situation with your health at around 38 years. You could have died.'

She thought for a moment. 'Yes. I was 38 when my husband attacked me with the knife. I ran away, though.'

In a drunken binge, he had lashed out at her with the closest weapon to hand. They were both Martian types, he being a negative type. Cuts and broken limbs are common health problems for this type, along with burns.

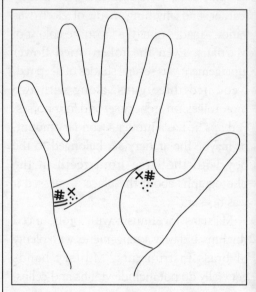

Figure 31 *Lines and signs detailing the negative Martian*

The negative Martian

Negative Martians can be recognised by a full mount of Upper or Lower Mars which contains a grille, cross or series of dots. Two or three horizontal lines on Upper Mars also confirm negative tendencies.

Negative Martians are frequently rough, violent people, and are sometimes abusers of drugs or alcohol. With very red hands they can be extremely sensual, and jealous to the point of committing murder.

With a large Lower Mars and very short

nails, these people are habitually argumentative. There is often little peace in their hearts and, as a result, those around them will have little peace. They can be magnets for trouble. This is the type of person who starts a fight in a bar which is then destroyed by a crowd of patrons.

Negative Martians are likely to be at the forefront in a riot. They can have difficulty keeping away from strife, often causing huge dramas. They are definitely not skilled negotiators. With a stiff hand, they can be slow and rigid, obstinate, unintelligent and quarrelsome. With a clubbed thumb (especially with short, broad nails) they have the potential to kill in a blind fury (see page 18).

I used to work opposite a married couple at a market. Almost every week there would be an almighty argument about how the stall should be positioned. She had clubbed thumbs and wasted no time 'going into bat' when a disagreement arose. Soon after she had won that battle, she would look around at the people on neighbouring stalls to see what differences of opinion were on offer. Many a morning I'd arrive to hear, 'Your stall space begins there and ends here! See that tree? It ends there, where that branch bends. Look, if you don't move it, I'm going to!' It would be the same argument every week. She would invariably win by being completely obstinate.

These people are best suited to fighting for a living. If they do commit murder, it is often a brutal, violent affair involving a knife, sword, gun or a blunt object which they use to repeatedly strike their victim.

As they have a strong constitution and an attraction to drugs and alcohol, they show stronger symptoms of negative behaviour when spoiled. Whereas the Lunarian gets drunk and falls asleep, the Martian drinks then goes in search of excitement.

A friend I grew up with had a negative Martian father. This man regularly beat his son with a strap, his fists and anything else available. One day when I was visiting, Derek's father laid into him for no apparent reason. I believe that all bullies are cowards underneath, so I decided to challenge him.

'That's enough!' I shouted, and he stopped for a moment. 'Leave him alone!'

'Look, you. This is my house and . . .'

'I don't care. There are two of us and one of you and you're pushing your luck.'

'Who do you . . .'

'Shut up. You're not my father and I owe you no respect,' I said, and began to tremble with fear.

He sized me up, and Derek suddenly stood tall and firm. We were both only 16 years old and I'm no wrestler, but he thought better of continuing and stormed out. I was still angry and outraged when I turned to Derek.

'Next time he starts, you're going to have to hit him. Once. Hard. Quickly. It's the only thing he'll understand.'

About six weeks later Derek did hit his father. Once. Right on the nose, breaking it. His father never bothered him after that.

Negative Martians 'get away with it' any way they can. Logic or reasoning rarely works with them. It's unfortunate, but often a bit of 'rough justice' does the trick.

THE MOUNT OF LUNA/THE MOON

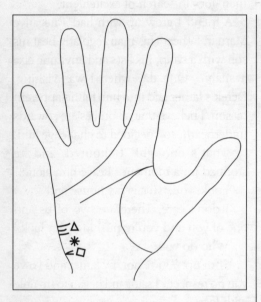

Figure 32 *Lines and signs on the Mount of Luna/the Moon*

The Mount of Luna, or the Moon, is located beneath the Mount of Upper Mars and above the Mount of Pluto. Traditionally, Pluto was included as part of the Mount of Luna. A full Mount of Luna which protudes from the edge of the hand confirms the Lunarian type. A triangle, square or star on the mount strengthens and adds to the Lunarian qualities. A whorl (a fingerprint-like pattern) in the centre of the mount also increases the strength of the mount.

Lunarians are usually tall, pale and anaemic-looking, with soft, bulging flesh that is spongy to the touch. They tend to have a prominent forehead and straggly hair. The eyes are round and watery and often bulging. The nose is short and small, sometimes a 'pug nose'. The mouth tends to be small and puckered. The teeth are long and yellow and usually uneven, the gums prominent (as distinct from the Jupiterian's prominent teeth). The chin recedes and the voice is high-pitched. The abdomen is large and bulging, the hips wide. They usually have flat feet and a shambling walk.

Most people who are interested in palmistry have at least a moderately developed Mount of Luna, as this mount increases a person's openness to the psychic sciences. Most people with psychic or intuitive abilities have well-developed mounts of Luna, Pluto and/or Neptune.

The Moon represents imagination. Communication is also represented — not the act of relaying information (as in Mercury) but rather the mode of communication (i.e. oral or visual communication).

Rigby is a classic example of a Lunarian. As he foraged around in the back of the cabinet for a bottle of 'the sherry drunk by the gods', I cast a glance around the room. Everywhere that a ledge existed, so too were books, cards and porcelain ornaments. It was a museum, library and bottle shop all in one. I wondered how he could drink so much and still survive, but soon my thoughts turned to other things as I noticed the tiny bell-shaped glasses still half filled with a honey-coloured liquid.

He re-appeared with a dusty bottle, two glasses, and a story of how he came to find this wine.

'It was a puncture — one which nearly killed us both, I might add — that led me down the lane in search of help in that dry, blistering heat. The heat in France gives one such a thirst.'

'Anything gives you a thirst, Rigby. Even drinking!' I laughed. Ignoring me, he continued.

'My French is appalling at the best of times, but I managed to convince the old man on the balcony that we were in desperate need of assistance. The wind whipped up a cloud of dust which threatened to smother me, so he invited me up to share a glass of this wine with him.'

'What about your friend back at the car?' I asked.

'I couldn't very well be rude to my host now, could I?'

'Are you telling me that you sat on a balcony in the shade drinking sherry with a stranger while your friend sat in the car at the side of the road?'

'I was in a state of shock or I never would have needed so much sherry.' His high-pitched laugh sent a ripple through his enormous body and for a moment I feared he might split the seams of his delicate waistcoat as he sprawled across the old lounge. His long teeth and prominent gums were visible each time he smiled.

'Exactly how much sherry did you drink while you waited for help?' I enquired.

'Not enough, I can tell you. I could have sat there drinking this until the vines encasing the balcony covered me completely. Of course, the cheese he provided was only to accompany the red wine he opened. I'm sure I refused at first, but continued refusal could have been misconstrued as bad manners, so I had to finish a glass or two.'

On and on he went about his travels, remembering each place vividly, often by the wine or the food, and building within me a great desire to travel again. The pale sherry was as good as he'd promised, and made all the better for the visions he created in my mind with his stories.

At the age of 56 Rigby remembered these events as though they were yesterday. I doubt if I could do as well after 12 years, especially with a wine cellar like his. He was a typical Lunarian, remembering life with a romantic flavour and relishing an opportunity to tell a story.

Lunarians are very imaginative, due to their slow lymphatic system. Because their bodies are choked up with waste, fewer nutrients reach the cells, leaving many Lunarians listless and sluggish. Although the physical body is slowed, the imagination is increased, for much sitting around gives them time to dream. It also requires very little energy to sit and dream.

Lunarians are frequently dreamy, sentimental and idealistic. They often have a great memory for the past (especially childhood) and sometimes live in the past.

I read for a Lunarian woman recently who

couldn't decide which of two paths to take in her life. Each offered promise and each held its own difficulties. To help her decide I asked her, 'Which of the two paths would you miss less if you chose the other path?' I accepted that she would miss that which she had not chosen, but suggested that, by choosing wisely, she could limit the feelings of loss which are ever present with Lunarians.

Although they are not usually good at nursing, they excel where nurturing is required. In a retirement home or when you need a bit of a fuss made of you, Lunarians are in their element. Both male and female Lunarians enjoy the home and love to cook and potter around. They generally love children and enjoy telling them stories.

Lunarians are normally restless, love to travel and can learn languages quickly and easily, especially when they visit a country as opposed to learning in a class. If they do not travel, they often dream of far-off places.

They usually enjoy the sea, rivers and lakes, preferring the view rather than the feel of water. To find the pure type in their natural habitat, simply visit your local beach at night when the moon is full. You usually find a few of them strolling about, staring wistfully off into the distance or watching the crabs. Cold nights do not seem to deter them.

Those with a full Mount of Luna can be moody, and around the full moon will often be bright, sparkling and unable to sleep at night. If they can sleep easily during a full moon, they often enjoy vivid dreams.

Lunarians can worry constantly. They tend to worry about not having enough money, security or safety, and though they may have little or no need to do so, they worry anyway.

A strong Mount of Luna can indicate someone who has idolised his or her mother or mother-figure. A push–pull situation can arise when these people reach puberty and want to seek independence but still feel a need to be close to their mothers.

Lunarian males are often quiet until around 14 years of age, when they suddenly become reckless and rebellious. This can continue until they are between 21 and 28 years of age. After this phase they often revert to being cautious and conservative, having resolved, to some degree, their relationship with their mothers.

The mother, or rather that which the mother represents, looms very large in the Lunarian's life. Many of the men find women enticing yet threatening, so they move from one relationship to another, giving little commitment but enjoying plenty of novelty. These men often marry someone with similar character traits to their mothers.

Female Lunarians are similar, finding commitment difficult and sometimes preferring to dream of a past lover rather than make the most of the present one. When the present partner is safely in their past, they can then love them in their own sentimental way.

Pure Lunarians tend to love you more when they have left you (or you have left them) than when they are with you. They are suited to being sailors, for this fulfils their romantic nature. The romance lies in the fact that their partner is often away in another place, and unavailable. If they settle, reality soon intrudes upon romance, and their restlessness surfaces again.

Lunarians love to collect such things as old books, records, photographs and memorabilia. They can be squirrels when it comes to furnishing a home. They love harmony in music and prefer soft, subtle colours when it comes to home furnishings. Soft pinks, lilac, pale blues and silver or silvery colours are Lunarian favourites.

These people are naturally secretive, for it gives a sense of mystery and this type loves mystery. They are superstitious (made less so by knotty fingers) and tend to be melancholic. They are 'night people'. Loath to rise early, they prefer to stay awake late at night for that is often when they have their best ideas and inspirations.

Lunarians love to write and to receive letters. They are amongst the great story-tellers. Whether it be making up bedtime stories for children, writing novels or simply exaggerating something that happened to them, they can entertain people for hours with their yarns.

Each year in the Lake District of England, a competition is held to find the world's biggest liar. Entrants must tell a tall tale in a convincing and entertaining manner to the crowd. The competition is held to commemorate the achievements of a local inn owner renowned for his tall stories. He works with liquid (a Lunarian career), tells tall tales, and works at night. All of these are Lunarian qualities.

Lunarians can be lazy, both physically and mentally. The pure types have to be pushed to become productive (unless they have firm hands and pink skin) and physical work can be distasteful to them. One Lunarian house maid on night duty in a hotel put it this way: 'Why should I work hard? Anything I leave unfinished will be done by the day staff in the morning.'

They can be extremely sensitive, especially to their own needs. They imagine slights when none are intended. They lack self-confidence and prefer to dream of success rather than physically attempt it, for in dreams disappointments can be easier to cope with.

Relationships

Lunarians, who are not an amorous type, match well with Saturnians, and are interested in but afraid of Martians. They can be too slow for Mercurians and a little too aloof for Venusians.

Lunarians often pair with Apollonians, but soon after they get together things 'go downhill' as Lunarians can find Apollonians different from what they imagined them to be. Lunarians match well with Neptunians, for both types have dreamy qualities. They are often attracted to the fire and enthusiasm of Jupiterians, but can dampen the Jupiterian enthusiasm in a relationship of any duration.

It can be difficult for the pure Lunarians to settle down with any one person, but they can have a good family life as they love children. Those with a full Mount of Luna can match well with a partner who has a prominent, low-set Mount of Venus.

Careers

Lunarians are often found in advertising, language schools, child daycare centres and working shift work. They can make good photographers, artists, writers and interior decorators. If they possess fine hands, they can be ambassadors, interpreters and translators.

These people are also attracted to sailing, whether a career in the navy or merchant navy, or simply working on or with boats.

Architecture and the printing industry are other career options for the Lunarian, along with working in bookshops or the hospitality industry. Because they tend to lack perseverance and enthusiasm, they are often not successful in business.

Working at night is another Lunarian preference — early mornings do not appeal to this type!

Health

Lunarians can have many health problems, some of which can be improved by regular exercise (not an attractive proposition to most Lunarians). Their slow lymphatic system benefits from regular exercise, which in turn improves their clarity of thought and physical health. If in good physical health, Lunarian types are more likely to pursue their dreams.

Lunarians tend to worry about their health and can become hypochondriacs.

They typically have delicate stomachs which spicy foods or worry can upset. Prolonged worry can cause stomach ulcers with this type. They also have a tendency to develop kidney and bladder trouble, gout and intestinal diseases, and Lunarian women can have womb trouble.

Rheumatism is shown by a large cross on the lower section of the Mount of Luna (just above Pluto) and gout as a similar cross in the upper section of this mount. Their poor circulation can give them cold hands and feet (shown by pale hands and little or no moons in the nails). They can be prone to colds and sinus trouble and often show an intolerance for dairy products.

Their glands also tend to function poorly and they can have strange-smelling perspiration. The tongue becomes coated and they develop a lot of mucus, leaving a bad taste in the mouth and throat. To reduce or clear this they tend to drink large quantities of liquid (e.g. coffee, tea, water), hence they have a spongy consistency to their flesh as they are literally waterlogged. Sometimes the liquid intake is low, but to compensate they eat watery foods such as fruit and soup.

The negative Lunarian

A prominent Mount of Luna which contains a grille, a large cross, several dots grouped together or a sloping Line of Head which terminates in a star on the mount can indicate a negative Lunarian person. Soft, spongy hands which are cold or moist add to the negative tendencies. At least three of the above signs must be present to confirm

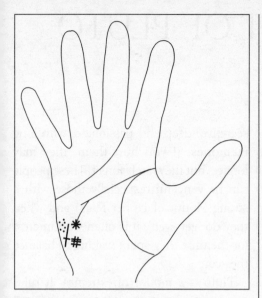

Figure 33 *Lines and signs detailing the negative Lunarian*

a negative Lunarian and not merely some negative tendencies.

Negative Lunarians are shorter than the positive type, with stiff, brittle hair and watery, grey eyes. Often the unpleasant odour of their perspiration gives them away, and they can also suffer with sinus trouble and catarrh.

They seek novelty in love and sex, but often have a reduced ability to give or to commit themselves to a partner. They are usually emotionally immature. Often negative male Lunarians are too busy running away from their mothers to commit themselves to one person. A sailor with a girl in every port is a typical example of the negative Lunarian.

They can be talkative and are some of the most vicious gossips. This type tends to be mean, selfish and cowardly. They can be deceitful and hypocritical, slandering those who achieve that which they do not have the courage to attempt.

I once worked with a negative Lunarian psychic reader who moaned all day about having to be at work by 11 am, grumbled if she had to give more than three readings a day, and complained loudly if she didn't have any readings.

This type can be slovenly in dress, moody and sullen, and will sulk at the slightest provocation. They tend to live on stodgy foods such as pasta, breads and anything that is cheap and filling. They can become overweight, as they retain liquids. They commonly fear failure in business and so opt for clerical work or work where there is a strong sense of routine, such as banking, secretarial work, typing and accountancy. However, they are usually not proficient at any of these, preferring to put in very little effort and dream the day away instead.

Negative Lunarians are morbidly superstitious. One Lunarian woman I know is convinced that when her relatives touch her they are filling her with negativity, and that certain rituals or being touched by certain other people will cure her of any 'bad energy'. In extreme cases the spoiled type can become lunatics; they can hallucinate and be unable to separate the imagined from the real, and then retreat into dreams.

THE MOUNT OF PLUTO

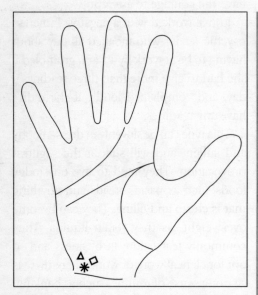

Figure 34 *Lines and signs on the Mount of Pluto*

The Mount of Pluto, situated in the bottom corner of the hand opposite the thumb and beneath the Mount of Luna, rules the deeper imagination. When this is the most prominent of all the mounts and contains a circle, triangle, dot, square or single vertical line, it indicates a Plutonian person.

Plutonians tend to have a long, beak-like nose and hollow cheeks. The eyes are often set wide apart and the hairline forms a widow's peak on the brow.

Plutonians have a penetrating stare which can be rather intimidating. They can give you the impression that they are looking through to your soul. They are usually secretive, deep and passionate, with long memories. If you hurt them, they may forgive, but they rarely forget. These people can be vengeful (especially those with a strong Mount of Upper Mars) and when they do 'get even', it is often with interest for the time they spent waiting to balance the score.

Pluto is a mount of extremes. It rules spirituality, obsessions, desires and the need to understand the causes of things. War, spying, drugs, psychology, psychiatry, detective work, research, ancient history, archaeology, anthropology, birth, regeneration, death, crime and sexuality are all in the Pluto domain.

Pluto also rules the shadow; that part of us we would often rather not look at and keep hidden from others. Plutonians are usually intense people, often obsessive, and they have a strong intuition. When meeting someone for the first time they tend to trust their 'gut feeling' about the person. If they decide that they don't trust or like you, no matter what you do or say, they are unlikely to change their opinion. They can be dogmatic.

Stephen taught psychic development courses for me some years ago, and when I was describing the Plutonian in detail to a friend, he laughed. 'You're describing my dad,' he said.

Some months later at a large convention for spiritual and psychic awareness, he introduced me to his father. I had heard from many people about this man. It was said that he was very intuitive, deep and direct. It was also said that when he met anyone for the first time, he would size them up in a moment, state what he saw, and treat them accordingly forever after. If he decided that he didn't like what he saw, you could forget about any niceties or polite chit chat. As he was the most respected person in the room of 300 people, it could be disconcerting if he disliked you.

When Stephen introduced me, his father stepped forward and shook my hand, all the while looking deeply into my eyes and into my soul. It was a look that pierced my very being, and it seemed to last forever. I broke out into a sweat immediately — no one has ever had that effect on me, before or since. Suddenly his face lit up, and the intense stare beneath those fierce eyebrows disappeared. He smiled with the same intensity as his stare, and he warmly shook my hand.

It is very hard to lie successfully to a Plutonian. They may not confront you directly, but they know. They are fiercely loyal to their friends and even excuse ill treatment from them once in a while.

Plutonians are similar to Upper Martians, except they tend to be more secretive. Theirs is a black sense of humour, often bitter, dry and understated — the actor/comedian John Cleese is a classic example.

Plutonians are attracted to the sea, particularly strong, turbulent seas, and often enjoy fishing, deep-sea diving and water sports — the Australian wine maker and yachtsman James Hardy is a typical Plutonian.

Owing to their calm, controlled exterior, Plutonians are very good at negotiating under pressure. These are the strong, silent types. They have immense courage and strong nerves in times of crisis. They can talk someone out of suicide while standing out on a ledge in gale force winds. It is usually a Martian or Plutonian who is called upon to defuse an explosive device, and it is also this type who probably set the explosives in the first place.

Plutonians have an interest in the past, and often trace their family trees later on in life. They usually prefer to wear black or navy blue.

Although they often hold many secrets, they are able to glean secrets from others easily. Other people often willingly confide in Plutonians, knowing that they can be trusted to keep quiet. Alison's mother heard all of her daughter's friends confessions and problems as they were growing up. Many of these teenagers felt unable to confide in their own parents, and came to rely on Alison's Plutonian mother for strength and an ear in times of crisis.

A strong Mount of Pluto indicates an ability to control crowds and groups of people. These people are usually charismatic. They can be great healers or great destroyers. They understand that to rebuild, sometimes you must first destroy. Either way they go about things quietly, not wanting to draw attention to themselves.

They don't give up easily, and this can make them relentless detectives and investigators.

An important lesson for Plutonians is that there is sometimes strength in surrender. Many Plutonians can find it difficult to surrender to the changes life brings them and, until they learn this lesson, there are few people to whom they will surrender. They prefer to control life. They sometimes choose to work with people who are experiencing great change as a way of becoming familiar with profound change in others before facing it themselves.

Life for the Plutonian can be a series of chapters. Distinct jobs, groups of friends and even locations accompany each chapter. Major changes usually occur between 48 and 51 years of age for these people.

Fifty-year-old Eva, who had suffered from bouts of severe depression and anxiety requiring medical supervision, experienced the Pluto change through the death of her father. Soon after, she divorced her alcoholic husband and set about improving herself. She completed a university degree and found a self-confidence she had never before experienced. She described the experience as 'Looking down the barrel at the rest of my life'. She did not like what she saw, so she changed it; once change had occurred, there was no going back and no desire to do so.

Bernadette was 52 when she came for a reading, and her strong Pluto mount made me ask her what changes had taken place during the past four years. Two weeks after her 48th birthday her mother died, and her husband followed some six months later. She moved house one year later and at 51 she had a hysterectomy. The age at which these things occurred and the type of health problem confirmed the Pluto changes.

Relationships

Plutonians partner well with Martians, Venusians and Neptunians. Because of their intensely passionate nature, some types are wary of them. Plutonians often demand loyalty and monogamy in relationships (although the negative types can be completely unfaithful) and if you break their trust you are unlikely to be given a second chance.

One Plutonian friend has an effective way of keeping her partner loyal. Whenever he starts a new job or joins a new club, she waits a few days, or even a few weeks, and then simply visits him. This visit has a dual purpose. It lets his co-workers or co-members know that she is his partner, and she has a chance to observe the competition.

Careers

Plutonians are suited to plumbing, research, psychiatry (with a well-developed Mount of Mercury or a straight, independent Mercury finger), psychology, police work, private investigation, spying, the building construction industry, journalism, the armed forces, motor racing, deep-sea diving and scientific research.

Peter, a private investigator, is the perfect example of a Plutonian. He visited me one day and, when leaving, drew my attention to a half brick which lay on the grass in the front garden. 'I wouldn't leave that there if I were you. It's the perfect entry device.' Glancing at the glass front door, I knew what he meant.

As counsellors or psychologists, they excel. Hypnosis is ruled by Pluto, as is an interest in past lives. Psychological nursing, geriatric nursing and hospice work are areas in which Plutonians can be found. They are attracted to working with the dying and those who are experiencing great changes in their lives. A well-developed Mount of Pluto is necessary for a surgeon, who needs 'nerves of steel' and steady hands when performing precision work in circumstances which make some people queasy.

Plutonians are suited to uncovering the hidden truth of any situation. Whether working as counsellors or journalists, they tend to seek the facts amidst the press releases.

Plutonians make excellent actors, due to the intensity of their feelings and their innate ability to focus on details. Character roles especially appeal to them. They remember past experiences with great clarity and the accompanying feelings are often communicated to an audience. Although they can be too intense on a one-to-one basis, they have enough emotional energy to fill a hall.

Health

Plutonians can have problems with the lower abdomen, bowel and reproductive organs. Constipation, lower spine misplacement and hysterectomies are typically shown on the Mount of Pluto.

These people have to be careful around alcohol and drugs, for they can display addictive tendencies. Obsessive-compulsive behaviour and addictions are ruled by Pluto.

A Plutonian friend once criticised an acquaintance for drinking every day, and then sat down to devour an entire packet of chocolate biscuits in ten minutes. Addictions vary. Some years back I rushed home to tell one of my co-tenants about an offer I had been made. I opened his bedroom door in a hurry and the door bumped his elbow. He was cross-legged on the floor with a syringe in his arm. 'Er . . . you look a bit busy right now, so I'll come back a bit later,' I said, and closed the door behind me.

The negative Plutonian

A prominent Mount of Pluto which contains a large cross, a series of dots or a grille confirms the negative tendencies. A horizontal line starting from the edge of the hand and running across to the Line of Life adds to these negative tendencies. This line is called a Line of Poison, and it confirms the presence of toxins in the body and shows a weakening of energy levels due to the toxins.

Negative Plutonians are frequently secretive, manipulative, jealous, possessive and unforgiving. If you hurt them, they cannot seem to hurt you enough in return. Sometimes they turn their destructive

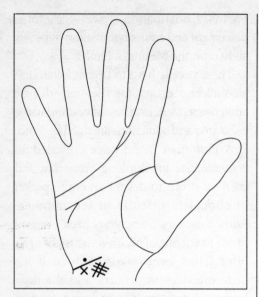

Figure 35 *Lines and signs detailing the negative Plutonian*

tendencies in on themselves, and when this happens they sink into depression.

Negative Plutonians can display an insatiable appetite for sex, drugs and alcohol, and dealing drugs or organising prostitution, running guns, smuggling, extortion and other underworld activities appeal to them.

Insurance fraud is common amongst this type, but pure Plutonian types are often the investigators, so they are up against their own type. The negative type can radiate an aura of seediness, sexuality and underlying aggression.

One negative Plutonian had an old car he had lovingly restored. It was stolen, set alight and pushed off a cliff after the thieves removed what they wanted — the motor. His insurance company refused to pay his claim, so he quietly set about organising his pay-out in other ways. He was the victim of several household 'robberies' which eventually equalled the value of the car plus interest. 'Personal grievance money' he preferred to call it. One morning I met him just as he was about to drive away. Our conversation went like this:

'Where are you going so well dressed?'
'I'm about to have an accident.'
'Oh?'
'Yes. I've got some rust in the back of the car and it needs to be cut out and repainted, so I figured five minutes on the main roundabout at about 10 am with a few sudden stops should fix it. Some mum will have just dropped the kids at school and will now run up the back of my car so my insurance company can do what I pay them for. The clothes? Well it wouldn't do to look too casual for an occasion as important as this.'

Negative Plutonians are often terrorists, whether behind closed doors in a family situation or through public acts of aggression. Memories of being powerless in some past situation can lead them to acts which are inappropriate in the current circumstances. Rather than confront you directly with a grievance, they prefer to kill the thing you love, often in a way that leaves you with no proof that they are responsible for the event.

Power is important to the negative Plutonian. A negative type was described to me recently by three men who sat beside me discussing their work. The conversation turned to politics, as they were senior public servants working under ministers in Federal

Parliament. A new minister had been appointed and they were discussing him. The older man laughed wryly and nodded. 'He was head of our department for six months about two years ago. It was a nightmare. He arrived, settled into his office, and then refused to sign anything for three months. Not a single order, letter, memo or document left his desk for 12 weeks. The whole department ground to a halt. He referred to it as "establishing ascendancy" and it was basically his way of attaining absolute power over the department and everyone within it. It worked.'

THE MOUNT OF NEPTUNE

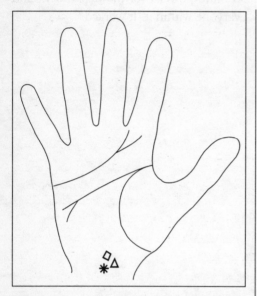

Figure 36 *Lines and signs on the Mount of Neptune*

Hands in which the Mount of Neptune is most prominent belong to Neptunians. A star, circle or triangle can increase the Neptunian qualities.

Neptunians have soft, oval faces and large, wide-set eyes. Their placid demeanour is often reflected in the almost child-like quality of their faces. The Neptunian face is one of graceful curves, as opposed to the bony, angular face of the Saturnian or Plutonian.

Neptunians are the most idealistic of all the types, ever hopeful that their dreams of life will be fulfilled. Neptune rules inspiration, and the Neptunians' task is to turn their dreams into something real. They are typically intuitive as well as imaginative. They can have a little trouble being practical, and are ever watchful for the tiny miracles along life's road. These people avoid arguments and can be dreamy and absent-minded at times.

They tend to love the arts, dancing especially, and enjoy the sea, rivers and lakes. To them, life is magical and practical things can get in the way. The following quote from Kahlil Gibran illustrates the type in a nutshell: 'They deem me mad because I will not sell my days for gold; and I deem them mad because they think my days have a price.'

Neptunians are often soft people, easily crushed and none too resilient to life's demands and pressures. If frustrated for too long, they may retreat into dreams. They are often extremely idealistic about life's possibilities. Those with a firm hand are able to push themselves to live out their dreams. They are often attracted to the colours purple and lilac.

They love animals, plants and all living things equally. I recall standing in a friend's bushy garden one day and, looking up, I noticed a small wooden box wedged into the branches of a tall tree. 'What's that up in the tree?' I asked.

'It's a box. It's a makeshift animal house.'

'An animal house?'

'Yes. There are a lot of creatures who might need a temporary place to live. The more the suburbs spread, the less space they have to make their home.'

It was a beautiful and practical gesture. It also made me aware of how much time I spent thinking about myself and my own life, and how little time I devoted to all the other species which co-exist in my neighbourhood.

The infinite patience of Neptunians seems to come from a belief that we are, each of us, doing the best that we can. They can be compassionate and self-sacrificing in their dealings with others, often displaying great sympathy for the weak or the underprivileged. They tend to gravitate to where they're needed most, and need to take care they are not exploited by others.

When I was in London, I took a stall at a charity fair in the grounds of a church. I read the palms of a couple of nuns, and one of them was a Neptunian. She was about 30 years old and showed a great compassion for children, the under-privileged and the frail. Her life plan was to work with street kids and orphans in the large towns and cities of Italy. She was not interested in progressing through the ranks or teaching in a school, but desired to work where she would be most needed. I can sometimes be cynical about the motives of people in religious orders, but this woman made me reassess my beliefs. Without the religion, the dress or the order behind her, she would probably still be helping someone, somewhere.

Relationships

Neptunians partner easily with Venusians and are attracted to the unfathomable depths of Plutonians, despite the dangers involved in exploring these hidden places.

Lunarians are another good match, for both are dreamy types and placid enough to leave one another undisturbed by too much change.

Martians often pursue Neptunians, but Neptunians find them too physical and passionate, unless the Neptunian has a secondary mount of Mars or Jupiter.

Neptunians can find a certain stability with Saturnians, but after a while a Saturnian will become frustrated at the lack of realism within a Neptunian.

Neptunians often find Apollonians attractive, as they make life seem grand, but unless an Apollonian can keep up such an affected pose the relationship is unlikely to continue.

Careers

Neptunians are often compassionate people, so any career which requires this quality, and is not competitive, suits them well. They are suited to nursing, counselling, helping others, painting and working with children or the underprivileged.

Oliver, a Neptunian, has had a wretched life, having been trampled on by those close to him. Both of his parents felt it their duty to put a stop to his dreamy tendencies and make him 'more suited to the real world'. With the best of intentions and the most brutal of methods, they left a legacy of fear and confusion which scarred him for life.

Now in his sixties, he can still find time for those worse off than himself. Working in the medical profession, he specialises in hospice work, displaying a great deal of compassion for the dying.

Religious and spiritual orders appeal to Neptunians, especially if they involve community work or support for the underprivileged. This type understands the true meaning of service to others and they usually possess great humility and are capable of continual self-sacrifice.

Clairvoyants, mediums and psychic healers are often Neptunian. Those with a full Mount of Neptune are not ordinarily suited to work that is repetitive or too practical, for their dreamy tendencies make them slow and sensitive. If forced into this type of work, they can develop health problems or sink into depression.

Dancers usually have a strong Mount of Neptune, as do poets. The movie industry (particularly animation) also suits Neptunians because it allows them to turn their dreams and fantasies into reality and, at the same time, allows others to dream with them.

Health

Neptunians can suffer problems with the feet, particularly cold feet (due to poor blood circulation) and corns. They also need to be careful that they don't hide from life through alcohol and drugs, for if life becomes too hard they are known to retreat into a dream world, assisted by drugs.

Neptunians can sometimes suffer from depression, due to restrictions from a partner or simply through life's circumstances.

Unless they have firm hands, Neptunians tend to experience depletion of physical and emotional energy. This is especially so if they work or live among people involved in emotional conflict. They absorb the worries and fears of those around them, and need time alone to recuperate.

The negative Neptunian

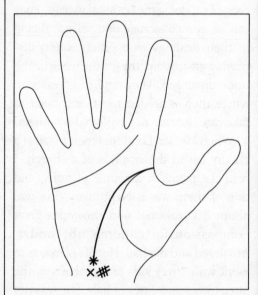

Figure 37 *Lines and signs detailing the negative Neptunian*

A prominent Mount of Neptune with a grille, several dots or an independent cross confirms the negative tendencies of the mount. These tendencies are increased if the hand is soft and moist, as those with soft, moist hands are less likely to make an effort to overcome their negative tendencies.

Negative Neptunians can be habitually self-deceiving, turning away from reality through drugs, alcohol or simply dreaming. Lomax considered himself to be a good father to Gene, an active three-year-old Martian. He would insist that his son stay overnight at his house each weekend and he'd pick him up from his ex-wife's home sometime on Friday evening, despite having agreed to be there at 4.30 pm. Once home, he would sit Gene down in front of the television while he spent a few minutes injecting himself with heroin. He usually spent the evening with his new partner, ignoring the child and endeavouring to remain awake.

In his mind, Lomax was a good father, for he wasn't shouting at Gene as his father had shouted at him. In a negative Neptunian fashion, Lomax was retreating from life and from reality.

Negative Neptunians can choose a life of martyrdom, sacrificing themselves and their needs to someone who doesn't appreciate the price they are paying. It can be a way of avoiding taking a chance with life, sparing them the pain of failure when their dreams are not fulfilled.

They are more of a danger to themselves than to others. They can turn their fears and resentments in on themselves and often suffer chest complaints, a lack of energy and vitality, or mild, prolonged depression.

Regular trips to the sea can balance them, if they are also prepared to tackle their fears and their dreams. I sometimes get the feeling that they are not completely present in their physical body. Their apparent vagueness can be the result of their mind being elsewhere.

Negative Neptunians can also attempt to lure others into their dream of what the world is like, by supplying the substance to which their friend or partner is addicted. In a loving way, the negative Neptunian can ensure a continuing co-dependence.

The negative type tends to live with 'the big dream'. The big dream involves a perfect life, soon after the lottery win or the inheritance or after the sponsor arrives. After the miracle, all will be well; however, a whole life is spent waiting for a miracle.

THE MOUNT OF VENUS

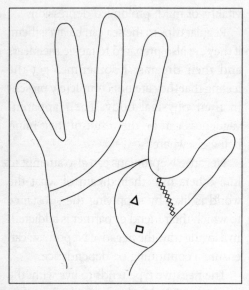

Figure 38 *Lines and signs on the Mount of Venus*

When the Mount of Venus is full and firm, and it is the most prominent mount in the hand, the person can be said to be Venusian. Venus rules love, sympathy and generosity. The typical Venusian is healthy and positive, and a man with a strong Mount of Venus (without a strong Mount of Mars) is usually a little feminine in his tastes and characteristics.

Venusians rarely have an angular body, it is more often a series of graceful curves. This type is the opposite of the Saturnian, who is bony, angular and aloof. When Venusians smile, dimples often appear in the cheeks and the eyes sparkle with joy,

love and sympathy. The mouth is beautifully shaped, with full, red lips, the lower lip being more noticeable. The chin is round and full, and often has a dimple. The hips are set high in both sexes. Because of the shape of their hips, Venusian women can experience difficulty giving birth; they do not possess the 'child-bearing hips' of the Lunarians.

This type seeks love, partnership and company more than any other type. When arriving for a reading, Venusians are more likely to turn up with a friend than alone. They are essentially affectionate. Love is rarely far from their minds and they enjoy all human contact, including friends, family and children. They are usually diplomatic, tactful and patient.

Venusians often have supple thumbs, which confirm their generosity towards others. In fact, William Benham, in his book *Laws of Scientific Hand Reading*, states that Venusians must have supple thumbs to be considered a pure type. I am inclined to agree with him. Steadfast in love, they consider 'we' and 'us' instead of 'I' and 'me'.

Venusians are typically exuberant, joyful and good company, which tends to make them popular. The pure type is unselfish. Venusians love the pleasures of life — good food, music and company — and often pursue enjoyment instead of money. They love beauty and harmony, both in their friends and in their surroundings. They are usually honest and truthful, and they forgive easily and are constant in friendship. They avoid quarrels and would rather accept an injustice than fight with others.

Venusians often possess a 'musician's thumb' (see page 19) and are able to play a musical instrument or sing. With strong Mounts of Apollo and Luna, this can easily be a musician's hand (depending on the shape, fingers and so on). Melody in music often goes straight to the Venusian's heart.

Venusian singers can put their heart into a song, moving the listener to tears or filling them with joy, depending on the song. At a party recently, a band was playing and various people took turns to sing their favourite songs. A man arrived in a pair of overalls which revealed arms covered with tattoos. He pushed his way towards the microphone, holding a beer and a cigarette. During the chorus, he burst forth with the sweetest voice I've heard in a long time. At the end of the song he smiled, and the tell-tale dimples appeared on both his cheeks. He was a Venusian.

Venusians are essentially positive in attitude. Their favourite colours are red and green, and those with a full, rounded Mount of Venus enjoy the sight of well-presented food. With a low-set Mount of Venus (full only across the base of the thumb, and not out to the Line of Life), they tend to prefer sweets, cakes, pastries and dairy products. Their good digestion contributes to their positive outlook on life.

Relationships

Venusians partner well with Jupiterians, Apollonians and Martians, and sometimes Plutonians. They could be matched with any other type and have a reasonably successful relationship, but Saturnians are likely to be too aloof for them and Mercurians too ambitious and busy.

They tend to partner well with a pure type which matches their secondary mount; a Venusian with a Luna secondary mount, for instance, is likely to match well with a Lunarian, especially a Lunarian with a Venus secondary mount.

Careers

Working with food appeals to Venusians, and it's sometimes hard to get into the kitchen when there is a Venusian around. They love to prepare and cook food as much as they love to eat it.

Years ago, I was sharing a house with a Venusian, and I was sad and melancholic over the break-up of a relationship. I arrived home from work to find that she had baked me a huge cake. Across the top in coloured icing were the words 'Happiness is a piece of cake'. It cheered me up no end. It was probably a Venusian or the partner of a Venusian who coined the phrase 'The way to a man's heart is through his stomach.'

A Venusian receptionist at the healing centre where I worked could often be found supplying complete strangers with tea and home-made cakes while they waited for their appointments. This woman used to say how lucky she was to live next door to several university students who appreciated her cooking. She would spend hours making a curry, cup cakes and a pudding, only to take it all next door 'to the boys'. 'They always seem so pleased to see me,' she said, beaming.

Venusians hate to see others unhappy, so any career in which people enjoy themselves suits this type. They are also suited to gardening, music and working in art galleries, as well as selling clothes, jewellery and beautiful things. They are usually happy with social work and nursing — anything where helping people is a part of the job.

In business and in life, they are usually better off in a partnership, as they lack the business mind of the Mercurian or the ambition of the Saturnian. They can be successful in catering, wine sales, chocolates or home furnishings.

Health

Generally, Venusians possess good health. However, they can suffer digestive trouble when negative, and neck and shoulder tension when the Mount of Venus is low set. Blue fingers or nails can signify heart trouble.

Venusians can have constant indigestion or a bloated stomach after eating, as the digestive system is their delicate area. This is confirmed by a Line of Health that is made up of many broken lines in a ladder-like formation (see page 157, Figure 104) and/or vertical ridges in the fingernails.

The negative Venusian

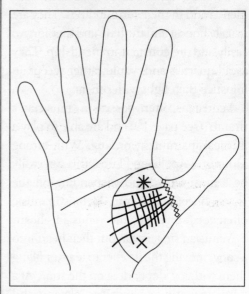

Figure 39 *Lines and signs detailing the negative Venusian*

A large grille on the Mount of Venus confirms the negative tendencies. Stiff thumbs and soft, flabby hands also suggest a self-indulgent nature which is at odds with the pure Venusian's generous nature.

Negative Venusians are easily recognised. The women often have a hoarse voice and both the men and women tend to over-indulge in food, drink and sensual pleasures. They can be self-indulgent (especially when the third phalanges of the fingers are thick and puffy) and can easily put on weight. They love food and often don't know when to stop eating.

Ronnie ate me out of house and home every time he'd visit. He was a bottomless pit. He simply couldn't bear to look at food without eating it. Most of a leg of lamb would be washed down by a bottle of red wine, with vegetables scoffed in order to make way for the biscuits he'd eat as dessert was being prepared. He'd drink a bottle of white wine to rinse away the taste of the biscuits, and eat a triple serving of dessert before opening a final bottle of red.

Negative Venusians can have trouble sticking to one relationship at a time. Sometimes they carry an ideal in their heads of what constitutes the perfect partner. If so, they constantly compare their partners with this ideal, and the partners, sadly, are usually found lacking. When the lower third phalanges of the fingers are full and puffy, there is a tendency for these ideals to give way to lust, and they constantly seek to fulfil their desires. Their entire energies are routinely given to the pursuit of enjoyment, even when others may suffer as a result of their actions.

Some negative Venusians can give out signals that they are available, yet act surprised when they are pursued. They can lack confidence and may need constant reassurance that they are desirable.

A FINAL WORD ON THE MOUNTS

Pure types are rare, so it is important to take into account the secondary mount when reading hands. I have devoted a great deal of space to the meanings of the mounts for the simple reason that not everyone has a palm covered with lines.

In a recent reading, a man presented a pair of hands with only four lines on each palm. There were no sister lines to the main lines and many of the usual main lines were not fully formed. Without a clear knowledge of the mounts and the back of the hands, my reading would have been over in a very short time.

The coarseness and firmness of a hand alters the meaning of the mounts: if you overlook this, you could end up being partially or totally inaccurate. For instance, a Saturnian can be expected to have firm, yellow hands, but a Venusian will not. A Lunarian with firm red hands is likely to be much more physically active than the typical dreamy, lazy, soft, white-handed Lunarian.

Many careers have been listed for each type, so check the fineness of the skin to determine the grade of hand before listing any possible careers. For instance, a Plutonian with coarse skin is better suited to plumbing, investigation or the construction industry than psychiatry or historical research. The secondary mount helps clarify the type of person. If you can't form a clear picture of a pure type, look at the careers listed and visit those places where you could reasonably expect to find them. Martians can be found at a football match or at a shooting gallery; Lunarians on the beach at night (or even in the day) during a full moon, or in an advertising agency; Jupiterians in a school or at a management meeting and so on.

No pure type is better than another, for they are merely different viewpoints of life. We need Jupiterians for their leadership abilities, Saturnians for their hard work and level-headed approach, Apollonians for their creative inspiration, and Mercurians for their communication and business skills. Martians offer us courage and tenacity, and Lunarians concepts and design. Plutonians seek the essence of humanity; our hopes and fears. Neptunians give our spirits wings to fly above the material world while Venusians remind us about love, companionship, sharing and friendship. Each type offers us something of true value, and I believe that the purpose of each type is to overcome its limitations and maximise its strengths.

A STORY OF THE MOUNTS

A man went out for a walk one day and he never returned. He walked across fields, alongside streams and over mountains. He walked for days and weeks and months, developing thick, strong thighs for his efforts. His name was Jupiter.

He laughed and learned as he walked, and he thoroughly enjoyed discovering new places and meeting new people. The first person Jupiter met was a very old man who questioned him about his journey.

'Where are you going?' the old man asked.

'I don't know yet,' Jupiter replied.

'Then why are you going?'

'Because going somewhere is better than being somewhere.'

'And when time has taken a little more of your life, where will you be then? And what reputation will you have earned for yourself?'

'Who knows?' laughed Jupiter. 'And who are you?'

'I am Saturn,' came the reply.

Jupiter continued his journey, walking all day before seeking shelter in a small village as the sun set. In the town square he met a juggler, who enlisted his help with a trick. Before the gathered crowd the two men juggled wands and brightly coloured balls, and together they enjoyed themselves as much as their audience. He had met Apollo.

'It is more than mere tricks,' explained Apollo. 'These people come to be entertained, and they walk away with full hearts and happiness. They take this happiness home to their loved ones. In this way the joy is shared.' Jupiter agreed, and the two talked late into the night.

The following day, Jupiter continued his journey. The days stretched into weeks, and the weeks into months. Summer gave way to autumn. Late one afternoon, he came across a short man in a cart. The cart seemed to be filled with his worldly goods.

'Where are you going with so many things?' asked Jupiter.

'I am going everywhere and yet nowhere,' came the reply. 'I am travelling around in circles.'

'In circles? Why do you travel in circles?'

'I travel this way because the things I buy in one place, I sell in another. When the people of the south have a surplus of leather footwear after a good year, it is cheap to buy. I buy it to sell to the people of the mountains in the north, for the cold always makes leather shoes valuable. When I have sold all my goods to the people of the north, I look around for things that are not available in the south and fill my cart again. I am always travelling and often I have a full cart.'

'I have walked far these last months,' said

Jupiter, 'and I could use some new shoes for my aching feet.' In a flash, the little man was standing beside him, holding a pair of shoes of perfect size.

'How did you know my size?' asked Jupiter.

'Practice,' replied Mercury. 'I have learned to judge a shoe size at ten metres in a matter of seconds.'

Jupiter purchased the shoes and continued on his journey. He bedded down for the night under a group of trees and quickly fell into a deep sleep. He was rudely awakened by shouting and dust all around him. He leapt to his feet to witness a man killing a wild bear in front of him.

With a pounding heart he stood by as the bear took its last breath and fell heavily to the ground under the man with the knife. This was how he met Mars.

'What on earth is happening?' he gasped when he could see that Mars had finished.

'I've been tracking this bear for three days now, and I only managed to catch up with it this morning. It was about to ransack your food supplies when I tackled it.'

Jupiter lit a fire while Mars cut the bear into manageable pieces. They drank a brew of strong tea and finished the last of Jupiter's bread with the honey which had attracted the bear, as Mars placed a few pieces of the animal's flesh on the fire.

'Do you hunt bears all the time?' asked Jupiter.

'No. Sometimes I hunt other, smaller animals, especially as the seasons change. I fish in the warmer months, but a bear like this one is a real treat.'

The next day, Jupiter continued on his journey. In the hot afternoon he saw the shiny reflection of a river in the distance and decided to take a swim. Alongside the river lay a man, deep in thought, holding a pen in one hand and a piece of paper in the other. Jupiter startled him as he approached the water's edge, and he sat awhile to talk.

'I was just wondering,' said the man with the pen, 'where the river might lead to, and who lives downstream. I wonder what language they speak down there, and what they think about before they fall asleep at night. I wonder what they dream of being, and where they dream of going. I wonder who lives upstream, and whether they think of things as I do.' The tall, pale-skinned man reclining under the tree was called Luna.

'Are you coming in for a swim?' asked Jupiter.

'No, thank you,' replied Luna. 'The water is too cold for me. It looks nice, but it's a bit wet for my liking.'

Jupiter found the water to be a perfect temperature, and he spent a whole afternoon splashing about to his heart's content. The next morning as he ate a hearty breakfast, Luna arrived again, to sit and dream, and to write letters to his friends, presumably downriver. Luna listened with wide eyes to Jupiter's tales of his travels and asked Jupiter to write to him often, telling him of the people and the places he was visiting.

Jupiter continued his journey once again, and the hills became steeper, with a colder wind and often a bleak sky accompanying him through the days that followed. It was a whole season before Jupiter encountered another person, and this man was deliberately situated where others would not distract him from his purpose. When Jupiter came upon him he was combining three types of powder, delicately, as though a wrong move would cause an explosion of gigantic proportions.

Jupiter stood quietly to one side, allowing the older man to finish his task, before starting a conversation. During the ten minute silence that followed, Jupiter promised himself that he would not speak until spoken to, as the older man seemed so focused on his task.

'Hello. I'm Jupiter,' he blurted out before he could stop himself.

The older man simply replied, 'I know'.

'How do you know?'

'I know.'

'What are you doing?'

'Shhhhhhh.' Jupiter fell silent once again, and the older man completed his work, grinding the three powders into a chalky paste with the help of a little liquid and a smooth stone. Jupiter had met Pluto.

Pluto was a patient man, not given to long conversations. He didn't talk much at all really, but Jupiter sensed that he knew a great deal more than he let on. Pluto finally spoke.

'History tells us that for many years man has sought the elixir of life. History also tells us that, in a few parts of the world, man found such a thing which, when used according to the texts, could help anyone who drank it live for a very long time.'

'Have you studied these texts?' asked Jupiter eagerly.

'No.'

'Then how do you know about the elixir?'

'I am my father's son. He was his father's son and so was his father. My great-grandfather knew this secret and, in the quiet of the still, summer days, I share his memory.'

Jupiter puzzled over this for a while, then Pluto continued.

'You are on a journey. This journey is nearing completion for you and a test approaches. You will be tested by the very thing which gives you the most happiness.'

'What will that be?' asked Jupiter, but Pluto was engrossed in his experiment once again and he did not speak another word. He had said all that he intended to.

Several days later, Jupiter met a delicate woman in the marketplace of a small town. She sat at a stall, selling beads, cloth and fine silks. She smiled as Jupiter passed her stall. Five times he passed her stall and five times she smiled at him. He stopped, pretending to browse, and she spoke softly to him.

'You are on a journey. Destiny awaits you, as she has awaited your arrival since she was very little, when she played on the swing by the gate near the old church.' Jupiter was surprised that she had spoken these words to him, and that she had repeated what Pluto had told him earlier.

'How do you know that I am on a journey?' he asked her directly.

'Some are on a journey and the rest are

waiting for the journeys of others to be complete. I, too, am waiting, but not for you. The man whose journey's destiny I am has only just begun his sojourn, whereas your journey is almost at an end.'

'And who is my destiny?' asked Jupiter enthusiastically.

'Her name is Venus, and she holds for you a gift. It is a small but priceless gift, which you will treasure above all else, and this gift you will one day give away, for it will become too big, even for you, to contain.'

'How do you know these things?'

'They are written. They are written in your face, in your smile and in your hands. Even your footprint carries a little of your secret destiny,' she smiled. That was how he met Neptune. They talked for a while, and she read his palms as the market closed.

Three weeks and four days later, Jupiter found himself striding hungrily through a quaint old town in search of a bakery. The previous night's dew was quickly disappearing from the roadside, and Jupiter was unaware that it was his destiny, not his hunger, calling him onwards. It was a Sunday and the townsfolk flocked to the local bakery as soon as the church service concluded.

Jupiter, eager not to be last in the queue, made his way to the front to be served. 'You look hungry,' said a young woman from behind the shop counter, with a smile which showed a perfect dimple in each cheek.

Their eyes met and they studied each other closely for a moment. They each experienced a strange recognition of the other. That small part of them which recognised that destiny was close at hand, told them to be alert.

He had met Venus.

Jupiter lost his hunger for food momentarily, as he satisfied his spiritual hunger. They fell in love immediately and lived together happily and peacefully ever after. Peacefully, that is, until the small but priceless gift arrived.

The gift was named Mars, and he screamed the house down for the first seven months of his life. Jupiter loved his little boy dearly but, as Neptune had predicted, his gift eventually grew too big for him to contain, and one day Mars set out on his own journey, to fulfil his own destiny, but that's another story.

Jupiter wrote all these things in his letters to Luna, prompting Luna to travel himself and to fulfil his own destiny with Neptune. Little did Neptune know that her conversation with a stranger by the name of Jupiter would lead to the end of her own waiting and the fulfilment of her destiny.

All things are connected, as Pluto will prove, if he lives long enough.

HUMOUR AS SHOWN BY THE HAND

From the moment I saw the red patent leather shoes, worn by the well-dressed man in the dark grey Italian suit, I simply had to have a pair. Big, hairy feet oozed out of the delicate ladies' shoes as he danced the mambo. My friend and I laughed so much we were almost in convulsions.

His chiselled face and proud stare blended perfectly with his suit, and I wanted to lend my black, sensible shoes to the woman next to me so that she could partner him.

I shared this man's bizarre sense of humour, and a macabre or bizarre humour is shown in the hand by an ulna loop (a fingerprint-like skin pattern) at the base of the Apollo and Mercury fingers, set between the two mounts. Those with an ulna loop laugh most when they need to let off steam, even at inappropriate moments such as funerals.

A friend of mine has a sense of humour that is a perfect example of this type. On one occasion, Rupert arrived for dinner at an exclusive restaurant wearing a pair of snorkelling goggles inside a diving face mask. In the space between the two, he had poured half a litre of water and four small goldfish. He nonchalantly ate his entree and sipped a glass of champagne while other patrons tried not to stare.

When asked why he was wearing a

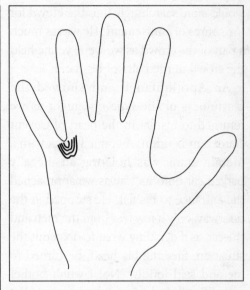

Figure 40 *An ulna loop on Mercury/Apollo, showing a bizarre sense of humour*

portable aquarium, he explained that 'The fish do so like to get out a bit, and having eaten here before I knew that the view could be improved a little. This way I have a sea view. Don't you find the sea relaxing?'

While I enjoyed Rupert's bizarre sense of humour, another friend preferred the slapstick humour offered by a juggler we encountered on the street. The juggler asked a child for the time, then feigned surprise when she lost her ice-cream as she turned her hand downwards to see her watch. Jupiterians often have a clumsy or slapstick sense of humour.

A Mercurian man had an audience in fits of laughter with his simple parodies. He would follow some unsuspecting person, exaggerating their mannerisms. When the person being parodied turned around, so too did the entertainer, and together they would stare searchingly into the crowd for the source of amusement. He was as much a part of the crowd as we were, yet he held the crowd in the palm of his hand.

An Apollonian friend showed the playfulness of the type one night as we returned to his flat in the heart of Covent Garden in London. A council truck with a mobile crane was hoisting an illegally parked car onto its tray as we approached the entrance to his flat. He stopped in the doorway, only a few feet from the men and the car, as if deciding what to do about the situation. Shaking his head, he turned to me and said loudly, 'No, I won't bother now. I'll collect the car in the morning.' We both fell about laughing at the expressions of the workmen, but only after we were safely in the lift. He didn't own a car.

A Martian friend sent me a letter, complaining that I rarely replied to her letters. To assist me in me reply , she included a page which read:

Dear Belinda,

_____

_____

with love, Paul

I responded with the shaky handwriting of a five-year-old, describing what I had done on my holiday. (The reply is Apollonian humour.)

Saturnians share an understated sense of humour, which can be so dry as to go unnoticed. Farmers often have this sense of humour. An old man explained why the crop had failed: 'Well, there was a drought. The drought ended though . . . the day the flood came.'

Plutonian humour can be rather black and often involves a power struggle. A perfect example of this is the Monty Python sketch in which John Cleese attempts to return a dead parrot to the pet shop.

Neptunian humour is gentle, often an observation of the foibles of human and animal nature. Venusian humour is also gentle, and a good deal more compassionate than Martian or Plutonian humour. Lunarian humour is often presented in story form, centred around clearly detailed, and often embellished, incidents from the past.

Part IV
The lines

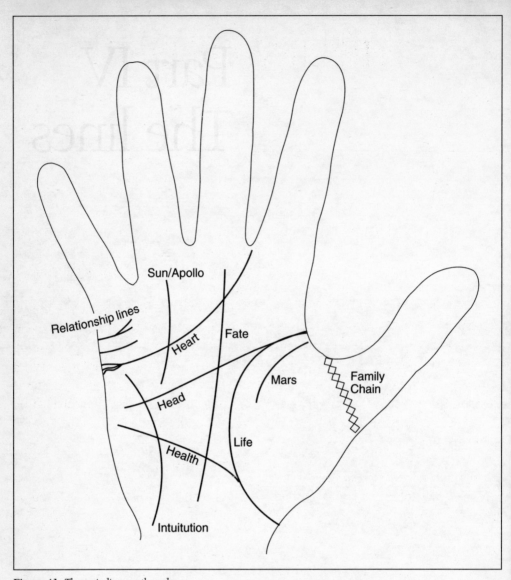

Figure 41 *The main lines on the palm*

The lines on our palms tell us about the dates and events in our lives. The non-writing hand is a guide to the past and the writing hand is a guide to the present and the future. Along with dates and events, the lines also confirm our qualities, and the length, position and direction of the main lines can reveal a great deal about character.

The reason the lines are examined after a close scrutiny of the mounts and the shape of the hands is that certain lines are normally found on particular shapes of hand. For instance, it is unusual to find a Line of Fate upon a spatulate hand, and if it is present, it has a greater significance than it does on other types of hands.

THE LINE OF LIFE

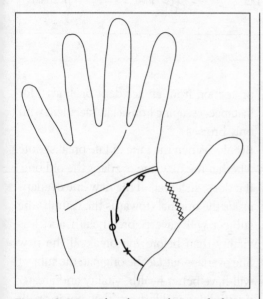

Figure 42 *Lines and markings on the Line of Life*

The first main line is the Line of Life. It deals with the quality of the subject's life, along with the approximate dates of events which take place — joys, heartbreaks, travels, relationships and illnesses.

The Line of Life can be described as a river. From above you see both its beginning and its end; you can observe all the obstacles to its progress, along with the opportunities for gaining strength and the flow from contributing streams.

As the line weakens, so too does the person's health and vitality. As the Line of Life changes direction, so too does the person's direction in life. When the line or river breaks up into many streams, so too does the person's life fragment into multiple directions.

The Line of Life starts where the thumb leaves the hand (between Mars and Jupiter) and curves around to finish at the bottom of the hand under Venus or on Neptune or Pluto.

If the Line of Life finishes under Venus, the subject will end up in his or her country of birth (or where he or she has spent most time). If it finishes on Neptune, the subject may end up in another city or country. Finishing on Pluto tells of finishing life far away from the place of birth.

Signs and markings

It is preferable that all the main lines appear deep, clear and free of dots, crosses, islands or breaks, as these markings impede the natural flow of the lines. But most people have several of these signs on the main lines, and their meanings are listed below.

Dot: A dot indicates an accident or illness, usually sudden. Check the Line of Head (see page 127) to see if any signs confirm the date. If so, it could be an accident to the head. If the Line of Life terminates at the dot, a sudden death is indicated.

Cross: A cross suggests a setback, illness

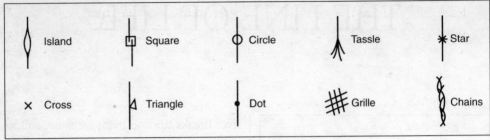

Figure 43 *Signs and markings on the palm*

or the like. If the Line of Life continues strongly after the cross, the person will recover. If a small cross appears inside and touching the Line of Life (see page 120, Figure 45), it can signify a legal case within the family; for instance, an inheritance divided between family members, legalities concerning a family business, or arguments within a relationship if it appears on one of the Relationship Lines. A tiny cross outside but touching the Line of Life indicates legalities involving strangers.

Circle: A circle on the Line of Life suggests eye trouble (check for an island on the Line of Heart under Apollo — see page 134, Figure 72) or simply that the person's life is going around in circles.

Island: An island on the Line of Life can detail illness or a lack of health and vitality while the island lasts. An short island at the beginning of the line can suggest a mystery surrounding the birth of the subject (e.g. adoption). A long island at the beginning of the Line of Life can detail a difficult childhood.

Square: Squares give protection wherever they are found in the hand. A square around a break in the Line of Life can signify protection from an accident or illness; for instance, escaping from a fatal accident with only bruises.

Break: When the Line of Life breaks, note whether the new line overlaps the old one. If it does, all is well. If the new line overlaps *inside* the original (towards the thumb) the subject will have poorer health and less vitality than before the break. If the new line overlaps *outside* the original, the subject will have better health, vitality and greater possibilities in life from that point on. It can also suggest that a move interstate or overseas will greatly increase the subject's chances of success in life. When a break occurs where the Line of Health crosses or meets the Line of Life, it can suggest a move for health reasons.

When the new Line of Life commences closer to the Mount of Luna or of Pluto (thus increasing the size of the Mount of Venus), life improves from that point onward.

When the Line of Life terminates and recommences further down the hand, it denotes a period of very little physical vitality for the subject until the new line starts again. It can, in some cases, signify the death of the person, but you must confirm this on other lines in the hand before you can give this meaning any validity. To confirm death, it also needs to be shown on the lines of Head, Heart and Fate, and if the Line of Sun is present, it could appear there also.

A couple entered a shop I worked in some years back, to inquire about a palm reading. She seemed very keen, but he was sceptical. I sensed that this was not a case of narrow-mindedness, so I asked him why he did not trust the science of palmistry.

'No reason,' came the reply.

'Tell him,' she urged.

'Tell me what? ' I asked.

It turned out that he had been given a reading when he was 28 years old, and the palmist had predicted that he would die at around 31 years. This was based on the break in his Line of Life at around 31 years of age. However, the palmist had not taken into account that a new Line of Life began outside the original one, overlapping it and continuing on its natural course.

I examined his hands briefly and confirmed that a big change did occur at around 31 years of age, but that he lived through it and had benefited from the change. His life had somehow improved, due to the positioning of the new Line of Life.

His wife explained that he had been involved in a car accident when he was 31. He had spent two weeks in a coma, but regained his health and became a new man.

'I mean it when I say that he is a new man,' she said. 'He was horrible before the accident. He cheated on me. He had a severe drinking problem and I had reached the point of asking for a divorce. But when he came home from the hospital he was a new man.' At this point the 'new man' was looking a little sheepish, but this did not deter his wife.

'If I'd known how much the accident would have changed him, I would have paid someone to arrange it sooner.'

Cross lines

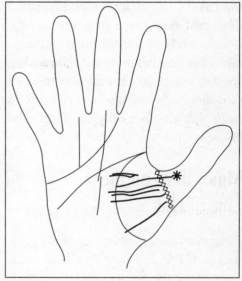

Figure 44 *Cross lines affecting the Line of Life*

Cross lines represent obstacles in life. When the Line of Life is weakened (thinned out) by a line crossing it, the subject's life force is diminished by the obstacle. When the Line of Life remains strong, the obstacle does not have any significant effect.

If the cross line originates from the Family Chain (see page 153), the obstacle will come from a family member. Repeated lines, beginning at the Family Chain, suggest that a family member wants to run the subject's life (e.g. an over-protective parent).

A star on the middle phalange of the thumb with a cross line running through the Family Chain and onto the Line of Life can signify the death of a family member. The timing is given on the Line of Life where the cross line reaches it (see page 126, Figure 59).

Sharon's hand showed two stars, connected by a line which ran out and crossed the Line of Life at age 11 or 12 years. I described how these two deaths were somehow related and she burst into tears, explaining how her mother had died when she was just 11 and her grandmother had died some eight months later of a broken heart, because her only daughter died before her.

Minor lines on the Line of Life

Often many minor lines are found alongside the Line of Life, and these lines detail events throughout the subject's life — travel, career advancements, family influences. Although tiny, they help build up a complete picture of the subject.

Little hair lines: When little hair lines are found drooping from or clinging to the Line of Life they signify a dissipation or loss of energy from the date which they appear. They are often found at the end of the line, indicating a loss of energy towards the end of the subject's life.

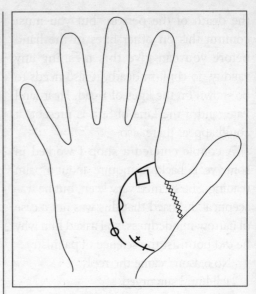

Figure 45 *Minor lines and signs on the Line of Life*

Travel Lines: Travel Lines are the little sister lines to the Line of Life, similar to the Relationship Lines (see page 158), except

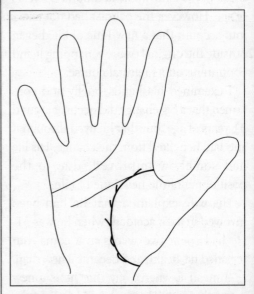

Figure 46 *Travel Lines and upward branches from the Line of Life*

they run alongside the Line of Life on the outside.

These lines do not suggest actual travel, but rather a restlessness for travel. Those with weak, flabby hands are unlikely to organise themselves to actually get up and do what is necessary to get going. They dream of far-off places, but do not arrive due to a lack of practical application.

A Travel Line that is long, clear and almost as deep as the Line of Life can suggest a move to another country, either permanent or temporary.

Upward branches: Lines which rise from the Line of Life indicate success or something gained at that point; for instance, a promotion at work (if confirmed on the Line of Fate), a child born, or successful travel if a travel line appears at the same time. They can also describe a move to a more suitable home environment or a time of improved circumstances.

When an upward line from the Line of Life ascends to the Mount of Jupiter, it tells of a great rise in position, or the realisation of an ambition. When such a line reaches the Mount of Saturn, there is likely to be a material success or gain. When it reaches the Mount of Apollo, it denotes distinction, according to the type of hand and the qualities therein. When it reaches the Mount of Mercury, and does not run into or cut the Relationship Lines, it indicates business or scientific success.

When an upward line cuts into or terminates on a Relationship Line, it usually suggests a divorce or a permanent legal separation (see page 161, Figure 110).

(Note: You can distinguish between an upward moving or a downward moving line by its thickness. It will be wider at its starting point.)

Friendship Lines: Friendship Lines are found on the Mount of Venus, inside the Line of Life and running parallel to it, but not touching it. They are similar to Relationship Lines, only not quite as close to the Line of Life, and can be dated in a similar way.

Dots on a Friendship Line indicate that the subject's friend is going through some shock or trauma. You can see the subject's age at the time the shock occurs (on the Line of Life), but not the age of the friend.

Friendship Lines which end in a fork show a fading friendship or a separation between the subject's friend and the friend's partner, especially when one of the Friendship Lines continues after the fork.

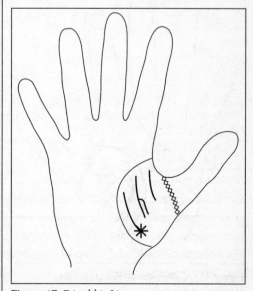

Figure 47 *Friendship Lines*

Pauline and Ruby became friends when they were 18, and a Friendship Line began at that age in Pauline's hands. Ruby's father died when Pauline was 21, and a dot shows on the Friendship Line confirming the shock experienced by Ruby (Figure 48–A). Pauline supported Ruby through a period of grief and they grew closer to one another (Figure 48–B). At this time, the Friendship Line moved closer to the Line of Life in Pauline's hands.

Ruby fell in love. A sister line sprang from the Friendship Line in Pauline's hands, confirming this (Figure 48–C). Ruby married and started a family. As a mother, she had less time to pursue her friendship with Pauline, and the Friendship Line on Pauline's palm began to move away from her Line of Life, confirming a fading friendship (Figure 48–D).

Some time later Ruby separated from her partner. The sister line travelling alongside the Friendship Line on Pauline's hand moved away from the Friendship Line and terminated (Figure 48–E). Once again Pauline supported Ruby, this time through her divorce. The Friendship Line on Pauline's hands moved closer to the Line of Life once again, as they grew closer to one another.

Ruby re-married, and Pauline developed a close friendship with both Ruby and her husband. Another sister line sprang from the Friendship Line and together these two lines continued to the bottom of Pauline's hands, indicating life-long friendship (Figure 48–F). While examining Pauline's hands, I could not judge what age Ruby was when these incidents occurred, but Pauline could relate to the events as I listed them.

How to date the Line of Life

To accurately date the Line of Life you will need a short ruler and a red, felt-tipped pen. A fine tip (0.4mm) is best so as not to obscure any tiny lines with the marks you are about to make.

It is essential to date the writing hand, and wise to date both hands. It is unreasonable to expect dates to be totally accurate, but if you follow the dating procedure carefully, you can expect an accuaracy of 18 months either side of any given date; an incident that you predict will occur at age 36 may actually occur at age 34 or age 37, for instance.

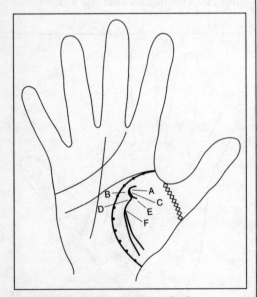

Figure 48 *Pauline's hands, showing her long friendship with Ruby*

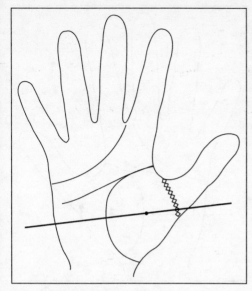

Figure 49 *Dating the Line of Life* (1)

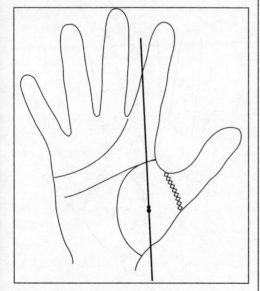

Figure 50 *Dating the Line of Life* (2)

Procedure

1. Place the ruler horizontally across the hand at the widest point (usually about the middle of the Line of Life) between the Family Chain and the Line of Life.

Mark the halfway point between these two lines with a dot.

2. Place the ruler vertically across the dot you have made and mark another dot at the halfway point between the Line of Life and the base of the thumb or the Line of Life, should it curve around beneath the Mount of Venus. Make it a little larger than your first dot. This dot is the mid-point between the Line of Life and the bottom of the hand. It is your main working point. Almost all future markings on the Line of Life will be relative to this dot. (Note: these two pen points are often very close to one another.)

3. Line the ruler up with the main dot and the centre point between the base of the second and third fingers. Place a small dot on the Line of Life at the point where the ruler crosses it.

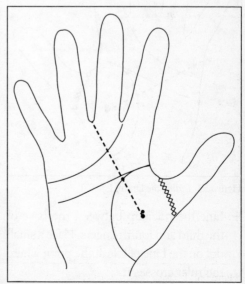

Figure 51 *Dating the Line of Life* (3)

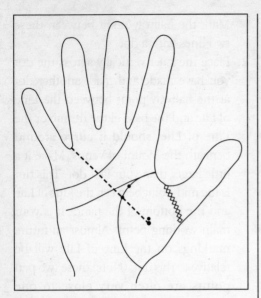

Figure 52 *Dating the Line of Life (4)*

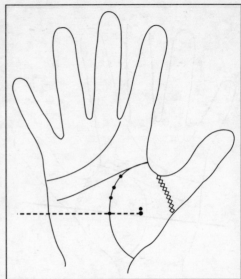

Figure 54 *Dating the Line of Life (6)*

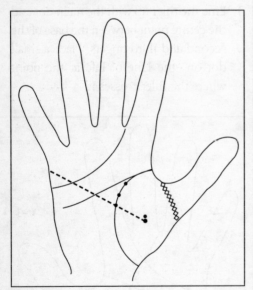

Figure 53 *Dating the Line of Life (5)*

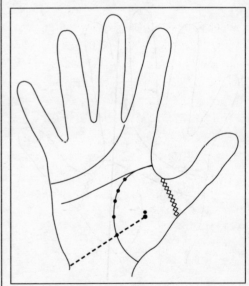

Figure 55 *Dating the Line of Life (7)*

4. Line the ruler up between the base of the third and fourth fingers. Place a small dot on the Line of Life at the point where the ruler crosses it.

5. Line the ruler up at the base of the fourth

finger, on the outside of the finger between where it and a fifth finger might be. Place a small dot on the Line of Life where the ruler crosses it.

6. Line the ruler up horizontally (straight

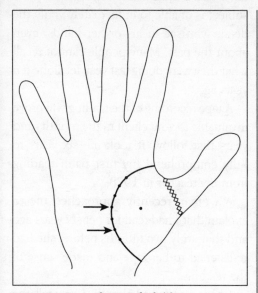

Figure 56 *Dating the Line of Life* (8)

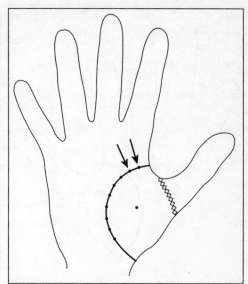

Figure 57 *Dating the Line of Life* (9)

across the hand) and level with the main dot. Place a small dot on the Line of Life at the point where the ruler crosses it.

7. Line the ruler up with the main dot and the bottom corner of the hand where the Mount of Pluto meets the first bracelet (or chain) across the wrist. Place a small dot on the Line of Life at the point where the ruler crosses it.

   You will now have five small dots on the Line of Life.

8. To these five dots you add two more dots. One in the middle of the space between the third and fourth dot; another in the middle of the space between the original fourth and fifth dot. You will notice there is a larger space on the Line of Life before the first dot.

9. Mentally measure the distance from the start of the Line of Life and the first dot. Divide this space into three equal parts, and place two dots on the Line of Life where you think they should be.

You will now have nine dots on the Line of Life, and each dot denotes a seven year period. The dots represent the ages of 7, 14, 21, 28, 35, 42, 49, 56 and 63.

10. Add a small line to the fourth dot to remind you where age 28 is. This will save you time later when you reach dates in the late fifties and find yourself counting each dot from seven years of age to confirm an event.

You may notice that the distance between the first three dots is greater than the distance between the last three dots. This is because the early or formative years have a greater effect upon our lives than the later years. For dates beyond 63 years, you can judge for yourself where the next dot or two

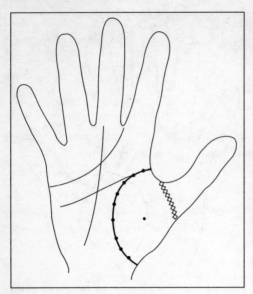

Figure 58 *Dating the Line of Life (10)*

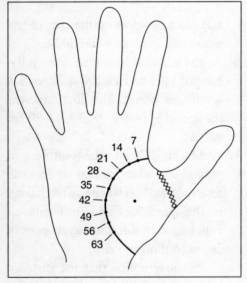

Figure 59 *Dates on the Line of Life*

should be, and each dot is still seven years apart.

You are now ready to begin with the birth and to proceed through the life, detailing dates and events. Don't be surprised if the subject is unable to immediately verify the details you see in his or her hands, even about the past. Many people cannot recall what they were doing last year, let alone ten years ago.

A tape recording of the reading will prove invaluable to your client in the months and years that follow. It took me six years to fully comprehend my first palm reading from my teacher in 1978.

A woman recently approached me to explain that I had read for her six years ago and that, only two months before, she had re-listened to her tape and made sense of the reading.

I have not found that you can tell the present age of a person by examining the hands, and I do not agree with those who suggest that a general reddening of the Line of Life at one point reveals the present age. Therefore, when you are reading someone's hands, it might help to establish in which year your client was born, so that you can give the timing in age and in years. For instance, for someone born in 1940, I might say, 'At around 35 years of age — that is, around 1975 — you formed a deep friendship which lasted until around 44 years, or until around 1984.'

Always start at the beginning of the Line of Life (the beginning of the subject's life) and move to the end. Try to avoid jumping all over the place as this increases your chances of leaving things out. Much of what you say can seem unnecessary or be forgotten at the time, but it can prove valuable later when your client replays the tape recording of your reading.

THE LINE OF HEAD

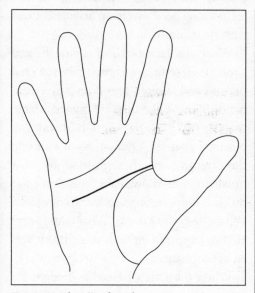

Figure 60 *The Line of Head*

The Line of Head depicts the mentality and the mental capability of the subject, A clear, strong line is a healthy sign. You can expect this line to vary according to the type of hand upon which it is found. The Line of Head can be dated using the same system as that for the Line of Heart (see page 132, Figure 69).

The Line of Head is like a river, flowing across the hand and directing the subject's mind towards a purpose. A creative or practical purpose is shown by this river's direction. All obstacles to the natural flow of this river are shown on this line, along with all assistance received. Like a river, the

Line of Head is better off flowing un-interrupted to its destination.

A strong, straight Line of Head, starting between the mounts of Lower Mars and Jupiter and reaching across the hand to the Mount of Upper Mars, indicates a logical, practical mind; someone who finishes what he or she begins. It denotes a practical, commonsense person.

When the line is chained at the start and appears to be tied down to the Line of Life, it indicates a person who was very much under the influence of his or her parents in the late teens and early twenties. The point where the Line of Head leaves the Line of

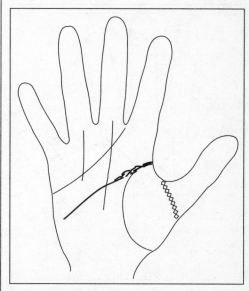

Figure 61 *A chained start*

Life shows when the person began to think independently. An example of this occurred in Geoff's hands.

Geoff's mother was ill, and had been for as long as he could remember. His father had walked out years ago and, at the age of 14, Geoff had taken on the responsibility of caring for his mother. She lay in bed, day after day, swallowing several large boxes of codeine tablets a week.

He became chained to her over the years that followed, and any time he went out of the house without her she would have a 'relapse' soon after his return. As a result, Geoff spent more and more time at home, until he could not bear it any longer.

When he turned 18, Geoff moved out of home, and around that time his Line of Head broke away from his Line of Life.

When the Line of Head starts on the Mount of Jupiter, independently of the Line of Life, it describes someone who thought differently from his or her family at a very early age. These people seem to understand that they have come *through* the family and not *from* it. They sense that they are 'just passing through', and in later life do not feel a strong need to remain in close contact with their family.

When the Line of Head is straight and short, it describes a thoroughly material person, and is often found on a spatulate hand. Bill was like this. He owned a large waterfront property and had various business interests. Over a glass of wine one day, he gave me his philosophy in a nutshell. 'You know, Paul, you think too much. I know enough to live comfortably. What else could I want?' What could I say? He was happy, so for him, this attitude was an appropriate one.

When the Line of Head is straight for

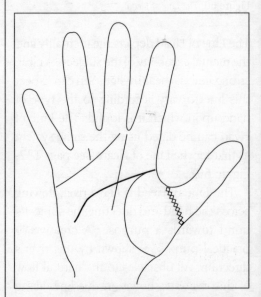

Figure 62 *An independent start*   **Figure 63** *A straight then sloped Line of Head*

the first half and then sloping, it shows a balance between the practical and the imaginative. This is often found on a conic hand. A straight line which ends in a fork tells of debating ability. These people are very convincing in verbal argument. They systematically tackle each point and don't give in easily.

When the whole line gently slopes towards the Mount of Luna, the subject is imaginative and more at home with creative things. This is often found on a philosophic hand. When the line slopes steeply, the subject is purely imaginative, romantic and idealistic.

When the Line of Head is gently sloping and terminates in a fork, it tells of painting or writing ability. It is often called a 'writer's fork'. These people often have a need to express themselves in some particular way. This need could manifest as keeping a diary

Figure 65 *A steeply sloping Line of Head*

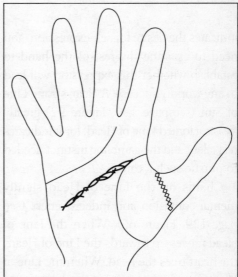

Figure 66 *A chained Line of Head*

or journal, painting watercolours at the weekend, writing letters continuously or publishing many novels or short stories.

Having a writer's fork does not guarantee success in any chosen artistic field, it merely

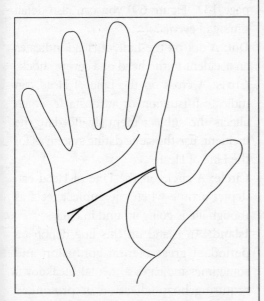

Figure 64 *A straight Line of Head ending in a fork*

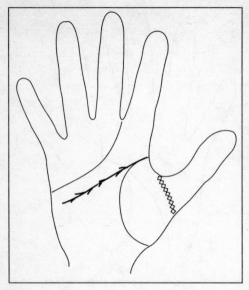

Figure 67 *Upward and downward branches on the Line of Head*

signify small goals which are achieved and their corresponding effects on the subject mentally.

When the subject has a Line of Head that is not 'normal' for that type of hand, the subject's character will vary quite significantly from the original description of the type of hand. For instance, a straight Line of Head on a conic hand (rather than the typical slightly sloping line) would give the person a much better chance of success in life as he or she will see a project through to its completion. It combines a creative nature with a logical, practical mind.

Signs and markings

When the following signs appear on the Line of Head you can relay additional information to the subject. Using the dating system as shown for the Line of Heart (see page 132, Figure 69) you can also detail timing of events.

Dot: A dot on the Line of Head indicates an accident to the head or a severe shock.

Cross: A cross on the Line of Head can indicate frustration or an obstacle which affects the subject mentally. To date the incident, use the same dating system as for the Line of Heart.

Circle: A circle on the Line of Head can depict a time when the subject feels as though life is going around in circles.

Island: An island on this line denotes a period of great mental confusion and sometimes indicates a mental breakdown requiring hospitalisation or prolonged medication.

indicates the desire for self-expression. You need to examine the rest of the hand to establish whether this expression will lead to any worldly success. A clear, strong Line of Sun (see page 149, Figure 92) greatly assists a forked Line of Head, for it indicates real talent and the gambling instinct needed to pursue such a career.

Chains on the Line of Head signify mental confusion and indecisiveness (see page 129, Figure 66). When the Line of Head moves up towards the Line of Heart, the heart rules the head. When the Line of Heart moves down towards the Line of Head (i.e. it is positioned lower than you would normally expect it to be on the hand), the head rules the heart.

Upward branches on the Line of Head take on the qualities of the mount they reach towards. Tiny upward branches

Square: A square on the Line of Head offers protection from breaks in the line at that point, or protection from the effects of a cross or an island if these signs appear inside the square.

Break: A break in the Line of Head where the old and the new lines do not overlap indicates a shcok or trauma which affects the thinking of the subject. If the old and new lines overlap, the break could indicate a change in thinking of the subject at that point.

THE LINE OF HEART

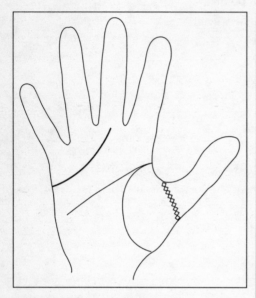

Figure 68 *A short Line of Heart*

'I suppose I'll ask the question everyone asks. You're probably bored with this question, but I want to know about love.' I hear this at least once a week from a client. My reply usually is the same each time.

'It's true that nearly everyone asks about love, because it's such a fundamental part of life. But I'm not bored with the question — if I become bored, it would be a very worrying sign to me.'

The Line of Heart does not predict love relationships or marriages. It does, however, describe the subject's attitude to love and, together with the mounts and the Relationship Lines, it can help you to determine the number and type of relationships the subject may experience.

The longer the Line of Heart, the stronger the heart's desires, or the more influence the emotions have in someone's life. The shorter the Line of Heart, the more important passion or physical desire is. It stands to reason that a medium length Line of Heart denotes a balance between idealistic and passionate love.

In hands where I have seen a very long Line of Heart, starting from the outside of the hand on the Mount of Jupiter, I've found the person to be intensely idealistic, often filled with disappointment at the shortage

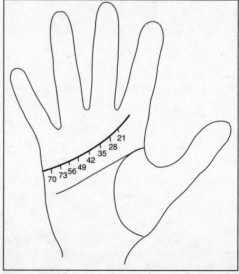

Figure 69 *A long Line of Heart; dates on the Line of Heart*

of noble intent or altruistic motive in others.

When I suggested to a client that she might place too great an emphasis on love, and that perhaps she put her partner on a pedestal, her eyes filled with tears and she softly said, 'No one has suffered the way I have.' She may have been right, but I wondered how much of her suffering was of her own making. When I see people like this looking for love, I sometimes think that they are looking in the wrong place. Perhaps they would be better off looking for a spiritual master to love, or someone, living or dead, who would not so easily fall from the pedestal. Perhaps they confuse unconditional love with the more realistic love that the average relationship requires.

The Line of Heart usually begins on the mounts of Jupiter or Saturn and terminates on the Mount of Mercury. The earlier the commencement or the larger the line, the more idealistic the subject is in love. The longer the line, the higher the subject's expectations in a love relationship, and the more jealous he or she is likely to be.

When the Line of Heart starts on the Mount of Jupiter, it depicts someone who seeks a partner of whom he or she can be proud. These people idolise their mate. When the line commences between the Jupiter and Saturn fingers, it denotes a calm, deep nature; someone who feels strongly, but balances this with thought. These people are more subdued than the previous type.

When the Line of Heart starts on the Mount of Saturn, the person tends to be more passionate and much less idealistic.

This type can be selfish, passionate and sensual.

A Line of Heart which begins under the Mount of Saturn and is chained and broad denotes a contempt for the opposite sex. I have never seen a Line of Heart that begins between the mounts of Saturn and Apollo, but such a line of would indicate an extremely self-satisfied person who had little regard for the feelings of others.

Breaks in the Line of Heart signify disappointments, heartbreak and despair. A break under the Mount of Saturn shows heartbreak caused by death; under Apollo, by pride; under Mercury, by foolishness. When at the start of the Line of Heart it droops down to the Line of Head, the subject has experienced some great disappointment or heartbreak in early life.

Marc was eight years old when he experienced heartbreak. He was ill, so

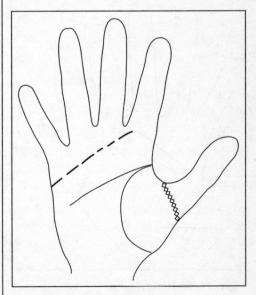

Figure 70 *Breaks in the Line of Heart*

missed out on a day trip with the family. When his mother and siblings left, he was confined to bed. He sat at the bedroom window watching his father in the garden. The dog wanted to play but his father was too busy. Eventually his father lost patience with the dog and went into the garden shed. He returned with a bowl of food, which he gave the dog. Unaware that his son was watching, when the dog's head was down in the bowl, the father produced an axe and brought it down across the dog's neck. He then buried the dog and told the family that it had run away. The boy never trusted his father again, and still has a Line of Heart which begins with a branch to the lines of Life and Head.

When the Line of Heart fades out, it describes a person who, through great pain or disappointment, has become cold and

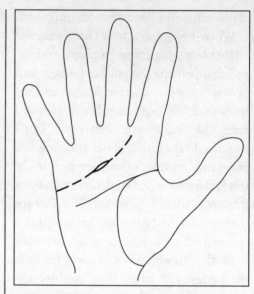

Figure 72 *A frail Line of Heart with an island*

careless emotionally.

Upward and downward branches at the end of the Line of Heart indicate the typical joys and sorrows of old age, along with a weakening of the heart in the final years of Life.

When the Line of Heart is joined by a line which stems from the Line of Head and runs along the Line of Heart, it indicates great mental and emotional confusion at the point in time where the line joins the Line of Heart. This confusion can include a nervous breakdown or a period of great moodiness. Decisions made during this time are less likely to be well thought out.

An extreme case illustrates the point. Some years ago, the chairman of a large corporation was made to retire early, as the company went through a period of restructuring. Although he received around $11 million as his retrenchment package,

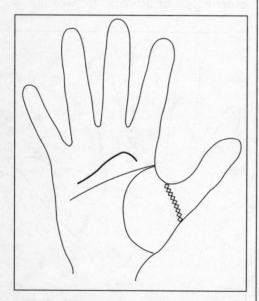

Figure 71 *The Line of Heart starting close to the Line of Head and fading out*

he rapidly sank into a state of deep depression and anger. Several months later, during a drinking binge, he sent his children next door to the neighbours' house during an argument with his wife. The argument escalated, and he struck his wife repeatedly on the head with a champagne bottle until she collapsed and died, whereupon he drained the contents of the bottle and walked into the sea, drowning himself.

Signs and markings

When the following signs and marking appear on the Line of Heart you are able to give additional detail to the subject about his or her emotional life, and in some cases, about the physical heart. The meanings are as follows:

Dot: A dot on the Line of Heart can indicate an emotional shock or a shock to the heart.

Cross: A cross on the Line of Heart indicates an emotional setback or frustration, often related to a love relationship.

Circle: A circle on the Line of Heart under the Mount of Apollo suggests problems with eyesight. If a circle appears in the non-writing hand, this problem is likely to be hereditary.

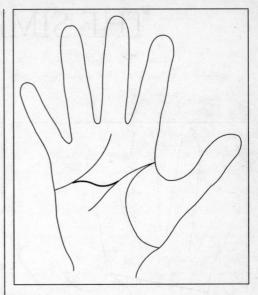

Figure 73 *A line running into and along the Line of Heart from the Line of Head*

Island: An island on the Line of Heart indicates a period of emotional confusion. If the island is under the Mount of Apollo it can indicate heart trouble at some point in the subject's life.

Square: A square on the Line of Heart offers emotional protection, especially if it encloses a cross or break in the line.

Break: A break in the Line of Heart has several meanings, depending on where the line breaks (see page 133).

THE SIMIAN LINE

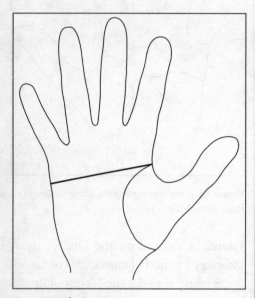

Figure 74 *The Simian Line*

The Simian Line derives its name from the fact that it is a characteristic of the hands of monkeys. It is a single line across the palm, a joined Head and Heart line.

To understand the Simian Line, you need to be familiar with the lines of Head and Heart. Both these lines have their appropriate position and territory on the hand. When the Line of Head moves up into the Line of Heart's territory, it comes under the influence of the Line of Heart; that is, the heart rules the head, or emotions tend to dominate thinking.

When the Line of Heart moves down close to the Line of Head, it comes under the influence of the Line of Head; that is, the head rules the heart. This is the case with people who think about how they feel instead of just letting themselves feel. These are the people who, as the house burns rapidly before them, think carefully about the most important thing to rescue while they still can.

Because the Simian Line is a joined Head and Heart line, you must decide whether it is in the position of the Line of Head or the Line of Heart before you can decipher its meaning.

A Simian Line in the position of the Line of Head describes someone who is rational, logical and in control of his or her emotions. Sometimes the emotions of such a person are suppressed completely.

A Simian Line in the position of the Line of Heart describes someone who is dominated by emotions. These people often cannot control their emotions long enough to gain a rational understanding of what they are feeling.

A Simian Line often indicates an imbalance between emotions and rational thought. If the Simian Line appears on the non-writing hand but not in the writing hand, then the imbalance between feelings and thought has been overcome. If the Simian Line only appears in the writing hand, look for a Line of Influence running

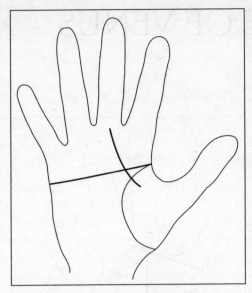

Figure 75 *A Line of Influence from Mars to Saturn crossing a Simian Line*

up into the Mount of Saturn from inside the Line of Life to see when the incident which caused the lines of Head and Heart to join occurred.

Talbot's right hand bore a Simian Line while his left hand showed separate lines of Head and Heart. The Line of Influence running from inside the Line of Life up into the Mount of Saturn crossed the Line of Life at 14 years of age.

I asked him what had happened when he was 14 that might have made him suppress his emotions so strongly (the Simian Line was in the Line of Head position). He thought for a while, as it was 45 years since the event. Then he looked at me gravely and nodded.

'I remember it well — too well. I lived in a small village in Poland. There was an old man in the village who was a tramp. I used to play in the sand hills just outside the village with a friend and, on this particular day, the old man was arguing with a younger man. I don't remember what they were arguing about, and the younger man stormed off. He returned about 20 minutes later with a rifle and shot the older man in the face — twice — killing him right in front of us. My friend and I were speechless. I'll never forget the madness that was visible in the young man's eyes.'

Perhaps, having seen what damage unchecked emotions could do, Talbot decided to suppress his emotions.

THE GIRDLE OF VENUS

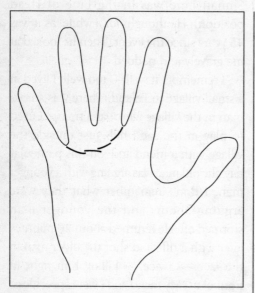

Figure 76 *The Girdle of Venus: broken lines*

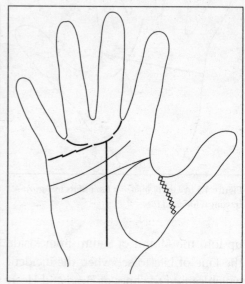

Figure 77 *The Girdle of Venus stopping the Line of Fate*

The Girdle of Venus is a line, or a series of lines, beginning between the mounts of Jupiter and Saturn, and cutting across Saturn to end between the mounts of Apollo and Mercury. It is almost a secondary Line of Heart. It can begin on the Mount of Jupiter, and can extend as far as the percussion, even cutting across the Relationship Lines.

Many extreme meanings have been attached to the Girdle of Venus. To understand this line we must look at what the Girdle actually does to the palm.

The Girdle of Venus cuts across the lines of Fate and Sun and the mounts. Before saying anything to the subject, observe whether the lines of Fate or Sun are weakened or stopped in their tracks by the Girdle of Venus. If so, the Girdle of Venus is likely to ruin any chances of the subject's success in life. If these lines are not stopped or weakened by the Girdle, then the effects of the Girdle are lessened.

There are two meanings that can be attributed to the Girdle of Venus, and the meanings vary depending on the type of hand upon which they are found.

People with a Girdle of Venus, a full Mount of Venus which is grilled or flabby, full lower phalanges on the fingers and a strong Mount of Pluto will be very sensual, and often quite perverted in their search for novelty of sensation. Their emotional scars from childhood have left them unable to give and receive emotionally without sexual and sensual overtones. This is especially so when the Girdle of Venus consists of many broken lines.

Those with a Girdle of Venus, long lines of Head and Heart, a flat Mount of Venus and thin lower phalanges on the fingers can have a heightened emotional sensitivity, making them idealistic and easily disappointed in love. They demand perfection of themselves and their partner. Once a fault is found with their partner, they often want to end the relationship or seek a way out.

I have often observed that people who have a Girdle of Venus can be very sensitive to criticism, both from others and from themselves. They can be perfectionists, giving up their plans and dreams at the first setback. They often lack tenacity.

The Girdle of Venus is about commitment, or the lack thereof. When you find a Girdle of Venus, look for a line running through the Line of Life to the Mount of Saturn. This line is called a Line of Influence. Where the Line of Influence cuts the Line of Life will correspond to a time in the subject's life, usually before 15 years of age. It indicates the age at which the subject made a very important emotional decision about life. This was the time when he or she decided that people were not to be trusted emotionally, perhaps as a result of a broken relationship between the parents; physical, emotional, mental or sexual abuse

from the parents or guardians; or simply a lack of emotional support and commitment from the parents. This decision can lead to a lack of commitment to self, loved ones and plans for the future.

Fiona complained that although she loved her children dearly, she resented the fact that they restricted her social life and her freedom. When questioned, she revealed that her mother often verbally blamed her and her brothers for preventing her from having a full social life, and even for ruining her mother's relationship with her father. Fiona seemed to be repeating this pattern.

These people seek someone to guarantee them commitment, which is impossible, and they invariably end up disappointed. They are emotionally immature; often functioning emotionally at the age when the

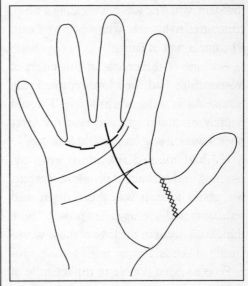

Figure 78 *A Line of Influence to the Mount of Saturn confirming an emotional decision about life*

decision was made. For instance, if a 13-year-old loses a parent, and receives no commitment or emotional recognition and support from the remaining parent, he or she could develop a Girdle of Venus, and continue to grow and develop physically and mentally, but remain at the age of 13 emotionally. You can imagine what this can do to attempts to develop meaningful relationships as an adult.

When I lived in London, I read for a man in his late forties who had a strong Girdle of Venus, and who was trapped in a relationship pattern characterised by a lack of commitment. His wife was committed to him, but he could not commit himself to her. He was involved in an ongoing affair, to which he insisted he was committed, with a woman who was committed to another man who would tie her up and whip her once a week in his cellar. In turn, this man, when he was not wielding a whip, committed to his wife, who was in love with a businessman in Paris.

Not one of the people in this chain of relationships had their love returned. My client said in a distraught voice, 'I would happily bind and gag and beat my lover once a week if she only would love me.'

He had missed the point entirely. Nothing in this chain of people and events was about love. It was about desire and sensuality and a struggle for power. These things can occur in the lives of those with a Girdle of Venus.

People with a double or triple Girdle of Venus tend to run away at the first sign of disappointment. All it takes is a tactless

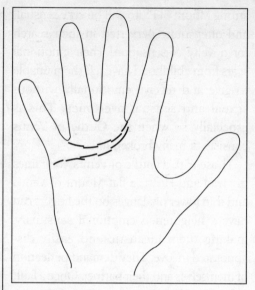

Figure 79 *A double Girdle of Venus*

comment, some criticism or simply a sign that a deeper commitment would be required.

An example of this is a woman in her early thirties who arrived on my doorstep for a reading, without an appointment, every three months. She was often hysterical and always pleaded for a reading. She did this on five occasions, and I was able to see her immediately or within two hours of her arrival, but on the sixth occasion I was completely booked up for the remainder of the day. I apologised, and asked her why she did not phone to book first.

'I lost your card,' she replied.

'What, all five of them?' I inquired, knowing that I had placed a business card inside the cassette case of each recorded reading.

I offered her an early appointment the following day as she seemed desperate, but by this time she had lost all interest as I had 'let her down, like all those before me.'

This had been her pattern from the time she was seven years old and, in the previous readings, I could not convince her to change or to resolve it. That would require work, of which she was afraid, or worse, commitment, which she did not have.

Even people with a single Girdle of Venus usually seek instant gratification of their needs. They seem unable to delay gratification or to work on a problem to resolve it, thereby ensuring long-term benefits. In this they are like children, who tend to react in a similar manner when faced with problems.

On another level, those with a Girdle of Venus can lose their personal power in relationships quite rapidly. They often have great difficulty loving someone without an exhaustive list of expectations or needs to be met in return. Instead of trying to perfect or improve themselves, they look for someone who is already perfect. They have difficulty setting limits within a relationship, and cannot seem to set and respect boundaries. Their reaction to a problem is to panic inwardly, or to run away. 'There is no problem so big that it cannot be run away from' can be their philosophy.

A heavily marked Girdle of Venus can indicate someone in desperate need of love, but often this person is not able to accept any love offered, for fear of dependence and disappointment. These people can crave emotional stability yet have a deep-seated distrust of those they love. They often show signs of what I call the 'picket fence syndrome': a desire for all external things to be neat, tidy and in perfect order, to compensate for their inner chaos. It is analagous to fanatically cleaning and re-painting a picket fence which is already in good repair. Meanwhile, within there is much cleaning and repairing required, but this is ignored.

For immediate relief of panic attacks or situations which have caused emotional turmoil, sitting in a deep bath, taking a swim in the sea, physical exercise or meditation can help. For long-term relief, these people need to work on the decisions they made at the age where the Line of Influence cuts the Line of Life on its way to the Mount of Saturn. A change of emotional patterns will take commitment and courage, which they must find if they want peace of mind and deep, loving, successful relationships.

Sometimes people with a Girdle of Venus avoid the colours green or yellow (i.e. the pure colours: nature's rich green and bright lemon yellow). If they avoid green, the problem is usually one of not having their emotional needs met. Music in the key of D, and raising plants and animals may help them to redress the imbalance, for theirs is problem with the 'heart chakra' or heart centre.

If they avoid yellow, the problem is usually one of personal power. These people can lose their personal power quickly in relationships, and soon find that they have given up their friends, their hobbies, interests and pursuits in order to meet all of their needs in one relationship. When the relationship ends, they are left with very little of themselves and their life, and they have to begin again. For these people, the outdoors, sunshine and exercise are required to return them to a balanced state, along with being surrounded with clean, cheerful yellows. Music in the key of E can also help soothe them.

A Girdle of Venus, especially a double or triple Girdle, brings out the negative qualities of the mounts it crosses. Across Jupiter, it highlights a desire for freedom; across Saturn, suspicion; across Apollo, a lack of relationship or ego boundaries; and across Mercury, indecision and dishonesty.

These people usually need to learn to love themselves. This requires patience, as it is often a long and painful process. Counselling can be helpful, yet it takes time to produce results, and these people are often impatient. In my experience, they are more likely to break appointments, turn up late or simply disappear without trace than any other type. They want a 'quick fix' or an instant solution to their worries and their moodiness.

To mirror their low moods, these people experience incredible highs. Who needs artificial stimulants when you can feel as high as these people do when something pleases them? Again, like children, they can become overenthusiastic, and from such heights there can be only one way to go — down.

They very often have an 'escape' plan; that is, even when they appear to be committed to something, they have planned a way out in case something goes wrong. It could be in the form of a bank account (one client kept a minimum of $95,000 as his emergency money), a second possible partner or a second job.

In times of old, people with a Girdle of Venus would have been suited to a monastic or religious life; an environment where they could access spiritual love, which would not disappoint them as easily as the love of a partner. This type of lifestyle would also have suited their quest for perfection.

At an ashram recently, I was able to examine the hands of some devotees of a spiritual master, and each hand I examined contained a Girdle of Venus. It is easier to love a guru or a spiritually evolved person. You're not likely to be woken up by a guru snoring in bed alongside you and a spiritual master won't usually leave the lid off your toothpaste. Less effort is required to love

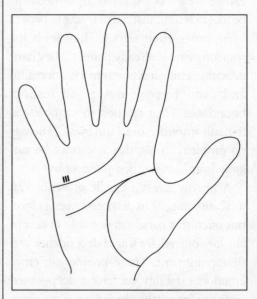

Figure 80 *Three vertical lines between the mounts of Apollo and Mercury signify pancreas trouble*

someone who is perfect or who is not present in your life.

A Girdle of Venus with three or more tiny vertical lines down by the Line of Heart between the mounts of Apollo and Mercury, can show trouble with the pancreas, such as hypoglycaemia or diabetes. In this case, blood sugar fluctuations may cause or contribute to mood swings.

A Girdle of Venus that is comprised of a single, unbroken line, running from between the Jupiter and Saturn fingers and ending between the Apollo and Mercury fingers can signify genius. These people have the desire for genius and the talent or ability to fulfil their desires. This line is very rare, and most Girdles of Venus are broken, giving the desire for genius without the ability to fulfil such hopes. A single, unbroken line will grant artists the ability to fill their work with their spirit, moving almost everyone who sees or reads it. This unbroken Girdle of Venus shows an artist of great talent.

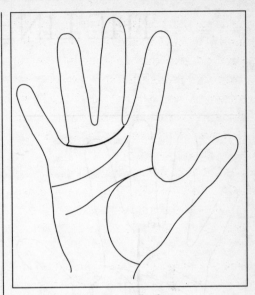

Figure 81 *An unbroken Girdle of Venus*

These people have, in effect, a second Line of Heart, giving them the ability to fill their work with love, purity and to make spirit visible in the physical form. They can still be temperamental, but they are able to finish what they begin more often than those with a broken Girdle of Venus.

THE LINE OF FATE

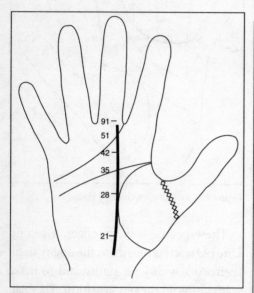

Figure 82 *The Line of Fate starting at Neptune; dates on the line*

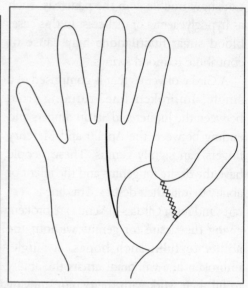

Figure 83 *The Line of Fate starting at the Line of Life*

The Line of Fate (sometimes referred to as the Line of Destiny or Fortune) has various meanings according to the hand upon which it is found. Spatulate- and square-handed people do not believe in fate so much as in hard work and careful planning, so a Line of Fate on these hands would mean much more than a similar line on a conic, philosophic or psychic hand.

The Line of Fate deals with worldly success. When it starts at the Mount of Neptune it tells of early ambitions. When it starts at the Line of Life it indicates that family members may have assisted the subject in starting his or her career.

When the Line of Fate is chained to, or held down by, the Line of Life, then chances are the subject's family held back or interfered with his or her early attempts at a career. When it starts at the Mount of Luna, it signifies that the subject is strongly influenced by another person or other people; for instance, the success of an actor is strongly influenced by the public.

When the Line of Fate starts at the Mount of Pluto, it indicates a burning ambition from an early age. Often these people have endured a childhood over which they had little control. Such frustration can breed ambition. These people have the ability to

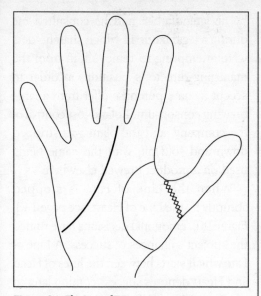

Figure 84 *The Line of Fate starting at Luna*

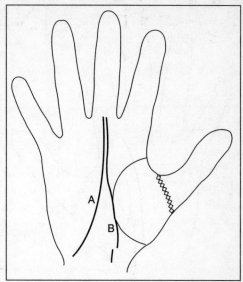

Figure 85 **A:** *The Line of Fate starting at Pluto;* **B:** *tied to the Line of Life*

control others and the desire to do so, even in subtle ways. They can draw upon the Pluto energy to further their career; for instance, an actor using Pluto energy to move an audience, a writer using this energy to research a subject, or a counsellor using Pluto energy to gently penetrate the defences of a client.

The Line of Fate usually terminates on the Mount of Saturn, suggesting a successful career, varying in success according to the type of hand (see page 148, Figure 91). On a psychic hand, the Line of Fate usually confirms a strong belief in fate rather than career success. On a conic hand it loses some of its importance, as conic-handed people are also often fatalistic. On a philosophic hand it often denote moderate success, while on a square hand it indicates a moderate to high degree of success. On a Spatulate hand it indicates that the subject is highly successful, as spatulate types do not usually believe in fate, but prefer instead to go out and create their own future.

When the Line of Fate terminates on the Mount of Jupiter (see page 146, Figure 86), the subject can enjoy enviable success in a leadership position; for instance, he or she may be a renowned surgeon, teacher, philosopher, religious figure or even a prime minister or a leader in his or her chosen field.

When the Line of Fate terminates on the Mount of Apollo (see page 146, Figure 87), the subject will be highly successful in creative fields; for instance, he or she may be an actor, writer, fashion designer, musician or anyone enjoying a level of notoriety. (Note: the Line of Sun also terminates on Apollo, and runs parallel to the Line of Fate. Make sure you don't get the two confused.)

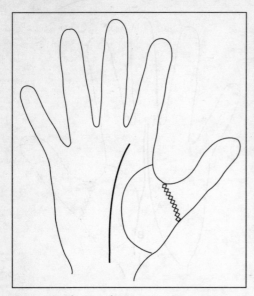

Figure 86 *The Line of Fate terminating on Jupiter*

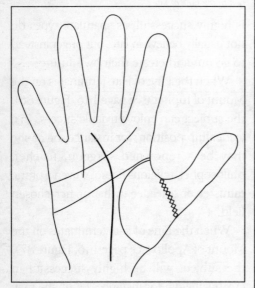

Figure 87 *The Line of Fate terminating on Apollo*

When the Line of Fate cuts into the Saturn finger, the subject loses control of the fate he or she had planned and destiny takes over. This was the case on Roland's hand. He was managing a brewery founded by his grandfather, and he consulted me during a legal battle in which shareholders were attempting to remove him from the managing director's position, in order to accept a share purchase offer from a large brewing consortium. Roland lost control of the company, and the plant was stripped down and sold off, with the name being used on a product brewed elsewhere.

When the Line of Fate is stopped abruptly by the Line of Heart (see page 148, Figure 90), emotional decisions have ruined the subject's chances of success. A Line of Fate which starts between the lines of Head and Heart denotes success coming later in life (from the age of 40 onwards).

When starting from the Line of Heart, success is quite late in life. Elaine, who had a Line of Fate which began at around age 46, left her husband when she was 45 and pursued a brilliant career. 'He was such a liability,' she laughed. 'I should have declared him as a tax deduction. He was merely an expense.'

Dating the Line of Fate

Using a ruler and a fine point felt-tipped pen, measure the Line of Fate from the rascette (the chain across the wrist) to the Line of Head and divide it into three equal parts, placing a small dot at each division.

The lower dot represents 21 years of age, the upper dot 28 years. Where the Line of Fate crosses the Line of Head represents 35 years of age.

Place one more dot mid-way between the lines of Head and Heart on the Line of Fate.

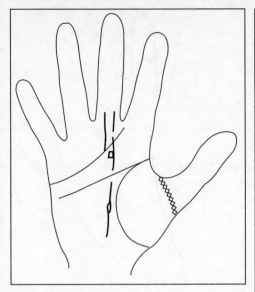

Figure 88 *An island, square and breaks in the Line of Fate*

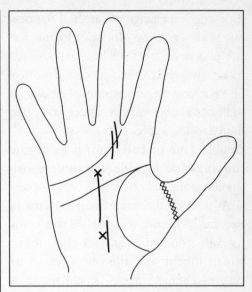

Figure 89 *Crosses and double Line of Fate*

This represents 42 years of age. Where the Line of Fate crosses the Line of Heart represents 51 years. The point at which the Line of Fate reaches the base of the Saturn finger is 91 years of age (see page 144, Figure 82).

Signs and markings

The signs and markings which can sometimes be found on or touching the Line of Fate have significant meanings, which are described below.

Dot: A dot on the Line of Fate indicates a shock or a difficult incident in the subject's career.

Cross: A cross on the Line of Fate indicates great difficulties in a career. If the Line of Fate terminates in a cross, it tells of a career destroyed or ruined, with little hope of career success from that point on.

Circle: A circle denotes a time when the subject's career is going around in circles. Little progression can be expected.

Island: An island indicates a period of frustration where little progress is made. It can describe unemployment or a time when the subject's career is stagnating.

Square: A square gives protection from difficult circumstances in career or in public life. If a break appears in the Line of Fate and this break is enclosed by a square, it indicates a smooth transition from one career to another.

Star: When the Line of Fate terminates in a star on the Mount of Saturn, it shows that the subject will enjoy great success in his or her chosen field.

Breaks: Each break in the Line of Fate tells of a setback. If the line breaks then overlaps, it describes a change of career. If the new line is closer to the Mount of Jupiter, the subject's new career will be a step towards more power and material success. If the new line is closer to the Mount of Apollo, it indicates a more creative career, and often more creative success.

Double Line of Fate: Two lines of Fate running side by side can denote two simultaneous careers.

As with all the main lines, the Line of Fate can be likened to a river. As you follow its path, you can clearly see the streams which join it and the obstacles to its progress. Some streams benefit the river, lending it extra force or purpose, while obstacles slow its progress or change its path. Sometimes enormous obstacles stop the flow altogether; at other times, similar

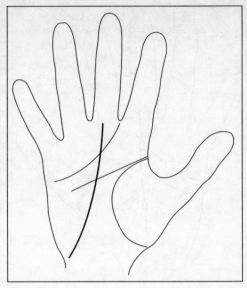

Figure 91 *A clear, strong Line of Fate*

obstacles slow its flow to a small stream.

Sometimes two rivers (careers) flow side by side, each being fed by tiny streams and, sometimes, by one another. The river flows with one purpose: to irrigate the Mount of Saturn, making the hard work of this mount bear fruit. The river (Line of Fate) knows its purpose, while the mount patiently awaits the life the river will bring. The Mount of Saturn knows that all things occur in time, and diligently prepares itself to meet the approaching opportunity.

The Line of Fate reaches the Mount of Saturn as a river reaches the sea, fulfilling its destiny and bringing with it knowledge of the journey. The Mount of Saturn makes practical use of the river's knowledge, turning it into something tangible, lasting and visible in the real world.

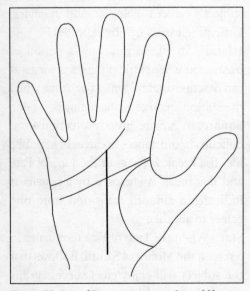

Figure 90 *Line of Fate terminating at Line of Heart*

THE LINE OF SUN/APOLLO

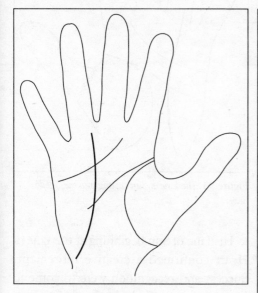

Figure 92 *The Line of Sun/Apollo*

The Line of Sun (or the Line of Apollo) is more often found on conic, philosophic and psychic hands, but it carries more weight on square and spatulate hands. It increases the success given by the Line of Fate, and brings fame and distinction. The system for dating the Line of Sun is identical to that for the Line of Fate. You don't even need to mark dots on the line, as a quick glance at the dots you placed on the Line of Fate will tell you at what age things occur on the Line of Sun.

The Line of Sun increases the Apollonian qualities and makes the subject keenly aware of the artistic. Where it commences is of great importance. When it starts at the Line of Life, the person devotes more time and effort to creative endeavours from that point in life onwards. When it starts at the Line of Fate, it increases the success of the subject from the point at which it starts. When it starts at the Mount of Luna, it brings creative success, determined by the tastes of the public. An opera singer I read for had this line. She relocated to Europe in order to achieve the success she desired. It was a difficult decision, but it proved worthwhile.

When the Line of Sun starts at the Plain

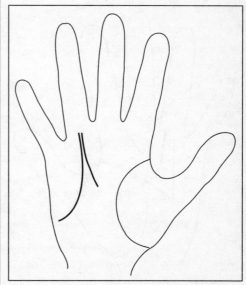

Figure 93 *The Line of Sun starting at the Plain of Mars and the Mount of Luna*

of Mars (see page 149, Figure 93), it brings success later in life. When it starts at the Line of Head, it shows that careful planning will bring notoriety and success, or that such success stems from the mind and the ideas it creates.

When the Line of Sun starts at the Line of Heart, or just above it, it tells of a creative and enjoyable old age. It does not suggest a great deal of notoriety or creative recognition, but instead a retirement spent pursuing those things which the subject finds fulfilling.

Daniel was 66 years old when I read for him. A banker all his working life, he was completely fulfilled in his retirement and able to spend long days in his garden. He spoke enthusiastically of the roses, the sweet peas and the scent of the jasmine which was beginning to blossom.

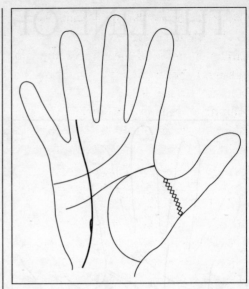

Figure 95 *The Line of Sun cutting into the Apollo finger*

His Line of Sun beginning at the Line of Heart confirmed a creative retirement. Success and recognition were to come to him on a smaller scale than to those with a long Line of Sun, as he was planning to enter his garden in the following year's local garden competition.

When the Line of Sun cuts into the Apollo finger, it indicates a gambler. This person will gamble not only with money, but with life, love, possessions and career.

Signs and markings

When the following signs and markings appear on the Line of Sun you can relate additional detail about the subject's creative or public life. The meanings are as follows:

Dot: A dot on the Line of Sun indicates a setback in the pursuit of creative goals.

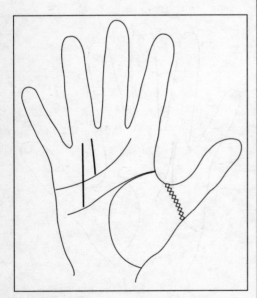

Figure 94 *The Line of Sun starting from the lines of Head and Heart*

Cross: A cross on the Line of Sun indicates an obstacle to creative goals.

Circle: A circle on the Line of Sun can indicate eyesight trouble if found on the Mount of Apollo.

Island: An island on the Line of Sun describes a scandal involving the subject, which lasts for the period of the island.

Square: A square on the Line of Sun offers protection, especially if it surrounds a break in the line or a dot or cross.

Break: A break in the Line of Sun indicates a period of less creativity or less recognition for creative endeavours. When a new Line of Sun overlaps the original line, it indicates a change in creative direction.

Star: A star on the Line of Sun is the most positive star in the hand. It depicts a life that brings brilliant and lasting success. Great fame comes with this star; the subject

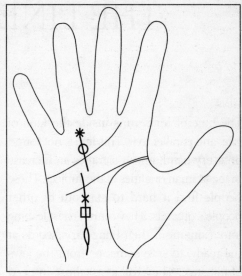

Figure 96 *Signs and markings on the Line of Sun*

may be a movie star, sports hero or public favourite, for instance. A star on the Line of Sun comes at a price, however, and the price of fame or notoriety is privacy.

THE LINE OF MARS

The Line of Mars runs inside the Line of Life, and parallel to it. This line is not found on every hand, and it signifies an increase in the Martian qualities of the subject. These people find it hard to stay out of other people's quarrels. They cannot resist leaping into a situation, their imaginary swords at the ready, to save someone from the jaws of injustice. They will assist those in need without invitation, and are sometimes surprised when those receiving their help don't appreciate the assistance.

The Line of Mars can increase the courage of an average person or make a courageous person adventurous. People with this line are more likely to champion a cause than those without. A hero in search of a crisis is how I describe those with a Line of Mars.

The Line of Mars has the added benefit of increasing the physical vitality and recuperative powers of the subject, making them healthier and less likely to be bedridden with disease. A strong cold or 'flu which passes through the community and knocks most people down for a week or two will only slow these people down a little.

When a Line of Mars is clearly visible in the hand, it adds strength to the Line of Life. The effect of any islands, crosses, dots or fading on the Line of Life is lessened by the Line of Mars.

The energy reserves of the subject lessen where the Line of Mars fades out, and he or she will be less likely to champion a cause in the years that follow. The age at which this occurs can be identified by dating the Line of Life.

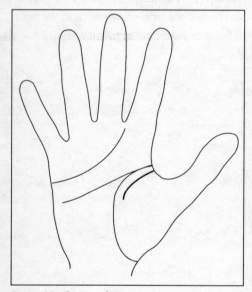

Figure 97 *The Line of Mars*

THE FAMILY CHAIN

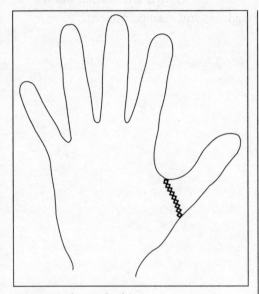

Figure 98 *The Family Chain*

The chain of lines on the thumb where it leaves the palm is called the Family Chain. The more chained this line appears to be, the more emotionally tied the subject is to his or her family. In the non-writing hand it relates to parents and siblings, and in the writing hand it relates to the subject's partner and children.

A thin, unchained line indicates a lack of emotional involvement or ties to the family. A noticeable break in the Family Chain details a period of separation from family. Angus has a break in his Family Chain, which reflects his experiences. He left home at 16 after being abused through-

out his childhood. He turned his back on his family for ten years, and although he has re-established contact, he is not emotionally close to them.

A Family Chain which starts at the Mount of Mars as a strong chain but fades into a single line, indicates a gradual diminishing of emotional ties with the family.

Lines originating from the Family Chain

Lines originating from the Family Chain usually indicate a parent who wants to live the subject's life for him or her. Interfering or bossy parents who seek to dominate their children give them a limited chance of making their own mistakes and gaining their own first hand experience (see page 119).

When these lines are accompanied by a strong Mount of Luna, the interfering parent is usually the mother. With a strong Mount of Saturn, it is often the father.

A 38-year-old woman came to me for a reading, bringing her mother with her. The daughter's hands showed many lines radiating from the Family Chain, and when I pointed out that one of her parents was probably dominating her life, her mother practically took over the reading.

'Tell her about the man,' she barked. 'She

doesn't want to know about family.'

'What more can I say?' I asked as our eyes met.

When the lines from the Family Chain cut the Line of Life, and slow it down and weaken it, the parent's influence is destructive. When a single line cuts the Line of Life and then branches upwards to the Mount of Saturn, along with a smaller downward branch, it can suggest an inheritance through the death of a relative. The upward branch tells of a material gain, while the downward branch shows the sadness and disappointment.

THE LINE OF HEALTH

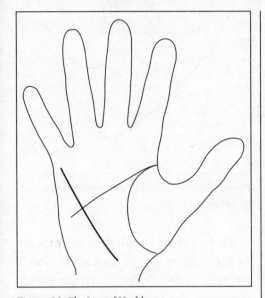

Figure 99 *The Line of Health*

The Line of Health (sometimes called the Line of Mercury) details the subject's health, in particular, the state of the liver. This line commences on the mounts of Luna or Neptune and terminates on the Mount of Mercury.

If the Line of Health touches the Line of Life it is not a good sign, suggesting an illness or even an early death, often due to the state of the liver.

A deep Line of Health indicates good digestion and a healthy liver, resulting in clear thinking and a reliable memory. Such a deep Line of Health can compensate for a thin, chained Line of Life in the same way

a Line of Mars gives added strength and vitality.

A chained Line of Health confirms that the liver and the stomach are not functioning properly. A heavily chained Line of Health indicates an advanced state of degeneration of the liver.

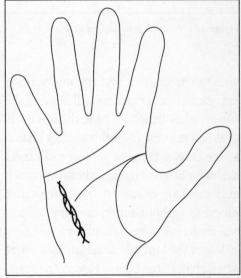

Figure 100 *A chained Line of Health*

This line can be dated using the same dating system as that for the Line of Fate. If the Line of Health starts as a strong clear line and becomes chained towards the Mount of Mercury, the health of the subject will decline in later years.

Bear in mind that this is one of the fastest

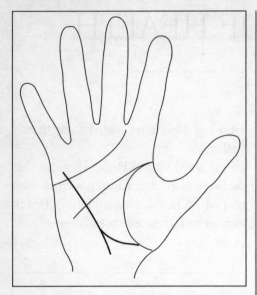

Figure 101 *A branch from the Line of Health to the Line of Life*

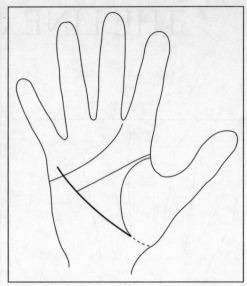

Figure 102 *The Line of Life terminates where crossed by the Line of Health*

lines to change, and that any intervention or positive health practices will improve the subject's health and, in turn, the line itself.

When the Line of Health sends a branch to the Line of Life, the subject can expect health problems at the age where the branch cuts the Line of Life. If the Line of Life proceeds without hindrance, the subject will overcome these difficulties.

When the Line of Life terminates where a branch from the Line of Health crosses it, it is likely that the subject's health will be severely affected at that age. With confirmation of difficulties in the other main lines at the same age (i.e. the other lines terminate at the same age), it could signify the person's death. It is important to recognise, however, that many people experience health difficulties in the later years and live to talk about them.

A wavy Line of Health details a tendency to suffer from bilious attacks or simply strengthens the health problems already shown by the type of hand. The health problems of the different types are as follows:

- **Jupiterian:** gout
- **Saturnian:** rheumatism and nervous disorders
- **Apollonian:** heart problems
- **Mercurian:** indigestion, stress on the nervous system and liver problems
- **Martian:** intestinal inflammation
- **Lunarian:** rheumatism and arthritis
- **Plutonian:** problems with the nose and the reproductive organs
- **Neptunian:** problems with glands and feet
- **Venusian:** problems with the kidneys and the digestive system

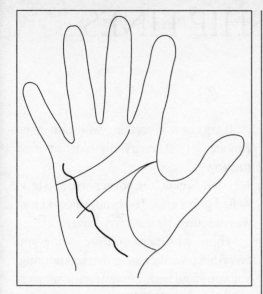

Figure 103 *A wavy Line of Health*

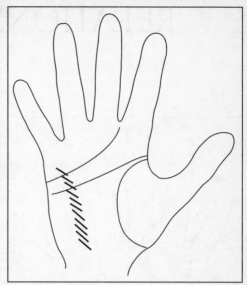

Figure 104 *A laddered Line of Health*

When the Line of Health forms a ladder, stomach and digestive problems are indicated. Digestive difficulties resulting from poor absorption of nutrients from food are confirmed by ridged nails (see page 27, Figure 12).

RELATIONSHIP LINES

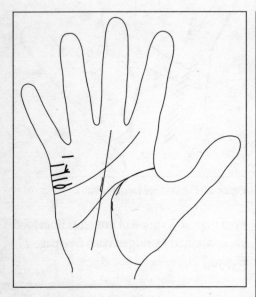

Figure 105 *Relationship Lines*

The horizontal lines starting on the percussion and extending across the Mount of Mercury are called Relationship Lines. There are usually several of these lines, but sometimes there may only be one. They are often referred to as Marriage Lines, but this is misleading as many love relationships can involve a deep commitment without a certificate of marriage.

These lines tell of love relationship opportunities, and it is up to the individual to refuse or pursue the opportunities that are offered. All relationships with others reflect our relationship with ourselves. The following story illustrates this.

'If you have everything you want, then why are you still hungry?' the old man asked the boy.

'I don't know,' the boy replied, and tears welled in his eyes. The beauty around him was obscured by his heavy heart.

'Those who raise you are giving you everything, yet they are giving you nothing. Still you stand here, hungry for the simplest of gifts — love.'

The young boy wept openly now, for the man had touched his hunger with gentle fingers and warm words of recognition.

The man sat cross-legged, gazing out over the lake as he spoke in a soft, clear voice.

'You must find yourself and love who you are, for in time, when you are grown, others will find you. When they do, it is essential that they find *you*, and not who you have decided to be. All relationships with others are in fact relationships with yourself.'

The boy's trembling fingers reached out and found his older friend's hand. They held hands as they gazed out across the lake. The wind was fierce but they did not notice. Their hands and their hearts were warm as they gazed, squinting, across the shimmering surface.

I find that many of those whose hands I read want to know what the future holds in store for love relationships. Sadly, I also find that many of these people have a poor or difficult relationship with themselves. It is reasonable to expect that a healthy relationship with yourself is a prerequisite for a healthy love relationship with another. My suggestion to those who are unhappy with their relationship prospects is simple: change yourself and the world will change accordingly.

The method of dating Relationship Lines is as follows. Divide the space between the Line of Heart and the base of the Mercury finger into three equal parts. The first division, closest to the Line of Heart, represents 28 years of age. The second division, closest to the finger, represents 42 years of age. The half-way point between the Line of Heart and the Mercury finger represents 35 years of age.

Before telling the subject the timing of the relationship opportunities shown, always check for confirmation of the

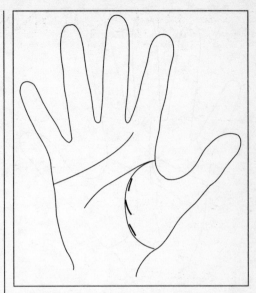

Figure 107 *Relationship Lines appearing as sister lines to the Line of Life*

relationship on the lines of Life, Heart, Fate and Sun.

On the Line of Life, Relationship Lines show as tiny 'sister' lines, running inside but parallel to the line. If these lines fade away (i.e. weaken and terminate), it shows the relationship has faded. If one of these sister lines end in a cross, it may signify that the relationship ends in divorce or a legal separation. If a sister line breaks and then continues, it indicates a break in the relationship. If the break is enclosed by a square, the person is protected from the full effect of the break. (Note: these sister lines can be dated according to the Line of Life, and therefore provide more accurate dates than the Relationship Lines on the Mount of Mercury.)

When the lines of Fate or Sun are strengthened by the relationship, as can be

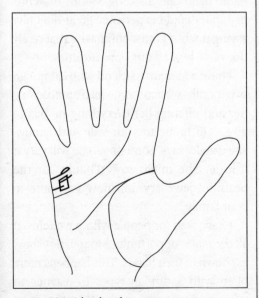

Figure 106 *A break within a square*

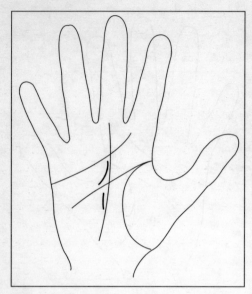

Figure 108 *Relationship Lines appearing as sister lines to the Line of Fate*

seen when a Relationship Line runs into these lines from the Luna side of the hand, making a stronger line, then this is a beneficial relationship to the subject's career (Line of Fate) or creative and public success (Line of Sun).

When Relationship Lines are strong and clear, the relationship will also be strong. When the line starts with a fork (two lines joining together to become one), it indicates a strong commitment following a period of independence or lack of commitment. When the line is weak at the start but becomes stronger, it shows that, although there was uncertainty at the beginning of the relationship, the bond has since grown and developed.

When the line is strong at the start but weak at the end, it tells of a loss of passion or interest in the relationship. When the

line ends in a tassle, it indicates utter dissipation and a scattering of affection. One woman with this line had lost interest in her partner over the years, and explained it this way: 'I feel as though he's married to his business. He works every night and most weekends, and when we are together he often falls asleep from complete exhaustion.'

When the line stops but is soon over-lapped by another line, it tells of a separation followed by a reunion (see page 163, Figure 112). When the line ends in a star, there will be an explosive finish to the relationship — the death of a partner, a violent ending or even an actual explosion.

Remember, Relationship Lines describe opportunities only, and if the subject is happily committed to a particular relationship when another presents itself, he or she has the free will to say no. Someone with a conic hand and a strong Mount of Venus or Jupiter could experience great difficulty saying no, but I must emphasise that rarely do we pursue all our opportunities.

I have a Mercurian friend who cannot go two months without some man approaching her and offering her everything he has to give. 'Go home to your wife and family,' she usually says. Sometimes she will vary it a little. She might say, 'Thanks for the beautiful jewellery and now go home to your family.'

I have read for people who have refused all the major opportunities for relationships as shown in their hands. This happens more often with Saturnian types (resistance to relationships), people with a Girdle of Venus

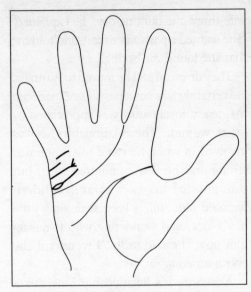

Figure 109 *Relationship Lines with a break, an island and a tassle at termination*

(quest for perfection), and with some Lunarians (sentimental attachment to a former partner).

Relationship Lines need to be compared with the other lines on the hand to ascertain whether the subject has any real affection for others. For instance, a Saturnian can have a relationship, but love is not the absorbing passion.

Broad or chained lines show indifference to love, and someone with these lines has no heartfelt desire to make a deep attachment to another.

An island on the line indicates some unhappiness during the course of a relationship. This unhappiness is often caused by a forced separation, perhaps a gaol term for one of the partners, a transfer overseas, or a period at sea in the case of sailors. If the island ends the Relationship

Line (see page 159, Figure 106), there is little likelihood of the couple being re-united.

Martin has several islands on his main Relationship Line, and he spent up to 18 months at a time in Asia, working on major engineering projects. When I asked him what his partner thought of the long periods of separation, he seemed surprised. 'I've never asked her,' he replied. His short Line of Heart confirmed his lack of thought for his partner's feelings.

If the Line of Relationship has a branch which ends in a star on the Mount of Apollo, the subject has an affection for someone brilliant and/or famous.

If a Worry Line (the horizontal lines which run across the Line of Life from the Family Chain) runs across the palm from the Mount of Venus, and cuts the Relation-

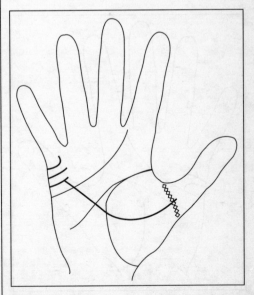

Figure 110 *Relationship Lines with an upward-turning line*

ship Lines, it shows that relatives are interfering with the relationship or marriage of the subject.

When a clear Relationship Line terminates in an upward turn, the person will not marry again. If a second Relationship Line appears, and it also turns upwards, it indicates that the subject will have another relationship, but will not marry again.

When a Relationship Line has many islands and little spots, it tells of great unhappiness in a lasting relationship.

When there is a fine line running parallel with and almost touching a Relationship Line, it describes deep affection for a previous partner. I recall reading for a man in his late thirties who was in a stable relationship of five years standing, who could not seem to shake off thoughts of his ex-wife and his children in England. 'My

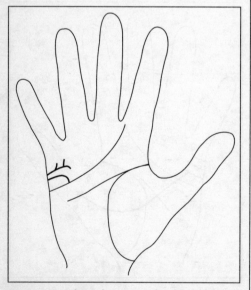

Figure 111 *Relationship Lines with a downward-turning line*

wife threw me out one day,' he explained. 'She wanted a passionate man, and told me that she found me boring.'

They divorced and he moved to Australia. He certainly was not a passionate man, but his steady, loyal nature was appreciated by other women. The relationship he was involved in when he came to see me was strong and he was committed to it, but thoughts of his ex-wife and children haunted him still. 'I keep seeing my little boy's face, and wondering who is raising him now,' he said sadly. 'I wonder if she ever married again.'

Alongside his Relationship Line was a sister line, which travelled half the length of the Relationship Line. As the sister line faded out before the main Relationship Line, I was able to tell him that he would eventually lose these intense feelings for his ex-wife, and enjoy his current relationship more fully.

When a Relationship Line bends down to and touches or crosses the Line of Heart, it indicates that the relationship will end in disappointment, and there may be lingering frustration as legal or material matters are sorted out. This is one of the signs describing a divorce.

When a second Relationship Line springs from an original line and runs alongside the first line, it can signify that a second relationship occurs at the same time, and is in some way related to the first relationship.

I once read for a man with this pattern who had an ongoing relationship with his partner's best friend, and for a woman who had a five-year relationship with her

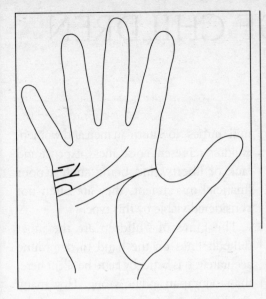

husband's brother. The fact that the second relationship line springs from the first one suggests that the second relationship springs from the first one.

In one case a woman told me that her ex-husband introduced her to her present partner some four years after they divorced. In her hand, the second Relationship Line moved away from the first line to become an independent relationship in its own right. It also appeared above the original line, closer to the Mercury finger.

Figure 112 *Relationship Lines with two lines overlapping, a forked line and a line terminating at the Line of Heart*

THE LINES OF CHILDREN

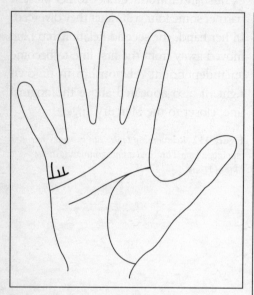

Figure 113 *The Lines of Children*

The Lines of Children are tiny vertical lines on the Mount of Mercury, above the Relationship Lines. Because they are so small, you may need to use a magnifying glass and a bright lamp to help you read them. The lines which show strongly represent children to whom the subject is close, not necessarily the subject's own children. Bear in mind that someone with a poorly developed Mount of Venus is less likely to have children than someone with a full mount. Saturnian types do not like children and, even in women's hands, children are less likely to show up, especially those born before the woman reaches her mid thirties. To Saturnian men and women, children represent noise, mess, expense and lack of liberty, and being such a poor financial investment, they are often not considered viable by this type.

The Lines of Children are the most difficult lines on the hand to determine accurately. It is better by far to be silent here, than to jump in and be wrong. 'How many children am I going to have?' is one of the questions a palmist is most likely to hear. I have learned never to answer this question unless it comes at the end of a full reading, and even then I point out that these are difficult lines to read accurately.

For greater accuracy, read only the children showing on the last Relationship Line, as these are more likely to be actual rather than possible children. Take your time before you decide how many children you can see. The necessity for caution is illustrated by the following story.

The mother of two energetic boys, Hayley had had a tubal ligation as she did not want any more children — the two boys were enough. They would have taxed the energy of even the most valiant of parents. Hayley went to see a palmist, who told her that should she choose to have a third child, it would be a girl. Hayley so wanted a daughter that she had the tubal ligation reversed and soon fell pregnant.

Hayley now has three boys. Admittedly, the third boy is soft and sensitive, but nevertheless he is a boy. The two older boys bully him constantly because he is disinclined to fight back, being a Lunarian type.

It is also advisable to read the Lines of Children only in private, as people become emotional when you detail the children indicated on their hands. We all have secrets, even from those closest to us. An example of this occurred with a friend of mine. I was visiting her at home, and her mother wanted a reading. I asked for privacy but she insisted that she had no secrets from her daughter. I took this at face value and gave her a reading in front of her daughter.

There was an uneasy silence when I pointed out that she did not marry the man she most loved, and she paled visibly when I mentioned the miscarriage between her first and second child. Her daughter's eyes widened and I had to speak up.

'You said you had no secrets from your daughter. Now we are all embarrassed.'

'But I never thought that it would be so accurate.'

I finished the reading with a bad taste in my mouth. I was young, but I learned that day not to allow others to witness a reading.

The Lines of Children indicate the sex of the children they describe. Generally, broad, straight lines indicate boys and thin, narrow, curved lines indicate girls. Sensitive boys show up as a thin, straight line, sometimes slightly bent, especially towards the end. Strong-willed girls usually show up as a strong line, but still with a slight curve or bend to it.

Twins show as two lines set close together (see page 167, Figure 116). This sign can also indicate a Gemini child. Once again, the lines are curved if twin boys, straight if twin girls.

The order in which the children are born is also indicated on the palm. The Line of Children closest to the percussion indicates the first-born child, the line closest to the Mount of Apollo, the last born.

When the line is clear, strong and unbroken, it denotes a strong, healthy child. When faint, the child is likely to be of delicate health.

When a line begins with an island, the child is in delicate in early life, or a late starter (see page 167, Figure 117). When this islanded beginning turns into a clear, strong line, it shows that the child will

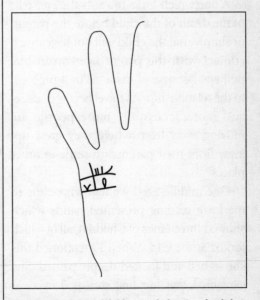

Figure 114 *Lines of children, including an islanded line and a forked line*

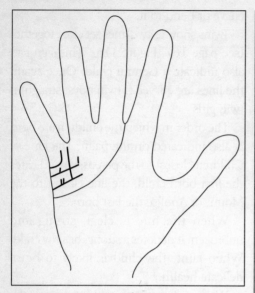

Figure 115 *Lines of children, which show a child who significantly affects the life of the subject*

AIDS virus when he was 23, and her daughter had moved to Europe to live with her new husband.

A different meaning occurred in the hands of another woman whose hands showed two Lines of Children, both of which forked at the end. When the children had grown up and left home, she divorced her husband and moved overseas, leaving them all behind.

A line which forks at its commencement tells of a miscarriage or a termination. The child is not born, or does not live long after birth (see page 165, Figure 114). I have found that when these lines show up in the past and the woman cannot recall a miscarriage, it could be that the child was lost in the first few weeks of the pregnancy, at a time when a miscarriage is not so easily noticed.

regain health or develop a sense of purpose in life.

A line which forks towards the end tells of the death of the child before the parent, or simply that the child will not have much contact with the parent later on in life, perhaps because of distance or a problem in the relationship. As travel becomes easier and more accessible, more people are moving away from where they grew up, away from their parents, to settle in other places.

One middle-aged woman who came to me for a reading presented hands which showed three Lines of Children, all of which forked at the end. When I mentioned this she sighed and looked deeply pained. She explained that her first son died in a car accident when he was 19, her second son died from complications resulting from the

A friend who had miscarried her first child was quite worried through the first months of her second pregnancy. I asked if I could take a look at her hands, simply for the purpose of examining the Lines of Children. The lines confirmed that a healthy boy followed the miscarriage, and that another two children followed the boy. Although I would not normally read these lines unless giving a full palm reading, I felt that both the child and the mother could do without 40 weeks of worry until he arrived. At the time of writing, this healthy little boy is 14 months old.

Lines of Children which extend right up to the base of the Mercury finger signify a child who has a deep and lasting effect on the parent. This child is likely to achieve a

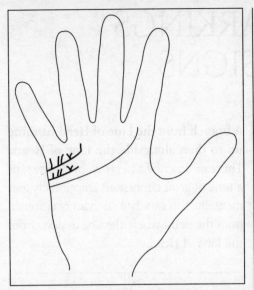

Figure 116 *Lines of Children including twins, a sign indicating a miscarriage or terminated pregnancy and a grandchild*

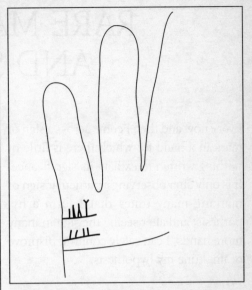

Figure 117 *Lines of Children detailing ill health in childhood and separation from parents in later life*

great deal in life, and often causes the parent to change his or her views about life.

When a line ends in an island, it can describe the child's death, usually after an illness. When one line is longer and superior to the rest, one child is more important to the parent than the rest.

On a man's hand, only the children he is close to will be visible. Usually, all a woman's children will show on her hand, for she has carried each child, and experienced the birth process.

A friend's mother lost her first child, and the doctor told her that she would be unable to have any more. She went on to prove him wrong, giving birth to ten children over the next 20 years. All 11 children show on her hands. At the time of the doctor's statement her husband was confused, because previously a palmist had predicted ten children for him.

Sometimes women who have never lost a child and are beyond child bearing age, may have a greater number of Lines of Children than actual children. This can be because they are close to someone else's child — a niece, a nephew, a friend's child or a grandchild.

Grandchildren usually are distinguishable as the space between them and the previous child is greater than the space between the first and second child.

RARE MARKINGS AND SIGNS

Every now and then I come across a sign or mark in a hand for which there is little or nothing written to explain its significance. It is only after observing a particular sign or marking many times that I form a hypothesis, and after seeing the sign in many more hands, I can safely confirm, disprove or fine-tune my hypothesis.

A short or absent middle phalange on the Mercury finger: This is usually the sign of a carefully guarded person. They are careful what they tell those around them, even those very close to them, because they are not sure of the reaction they might receive. This is usually the result of being the child of an unpredictable parent or guardian; for instance, the son or daughter of an alcoholic, a manic depressive or an easily irritated parent.

Eight-year-old Simon spent four hours pacing nervously about the house awaiting the arrival of his father after accidentally cracking a light shade while playing with his ball inside. He described his mother's reaction as being very similar. She cleaned nervously and planned a diversion for her husband, so that he wouldn't notice the damage Simon had caused. The man was given to irrational rages if things did not go according to plan, and breakages were never acceptable.

A branch from the Line of Head running up to then alongside the Line of Heart: This can describe a nervous breakdown or a time of great confusion, emotionally and mentally. You can date such an occurrence from the point where the line departs from the Line of Head.

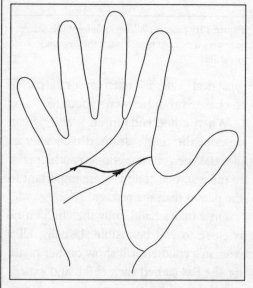

Figure 118 *An example of great mental and emotional stress*

Tina confirmed that she had suffered a period of depression between the ages of 21 and 25, which showed as an island on her Line of Head at 21 years and a line running from the Line of Head to the Line of Heart at the same point. After removing

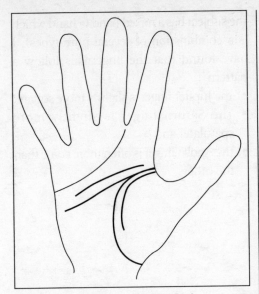

Figure 119 *Double lines of Head and Life*

A double Line of Head can also describe those who are able to use one side of their nature in business and the other side in their private life. Cecile is a successful lawyer by day and an artist in the evenings. Regular trips to the US for legal purposes allow her to arrange exhibitions of her work. Her double lines of Head and Fate, side by side, show success in two careers at once.

In a negative hand (see Part III), a double Line of Head can describe two distinct parts of the person's life which are kept apart.

Richard confessed that his wife and family knew nothing of his other family living in another city. He was a successful businessman who supported a wife with two daughters and a son, and a de facto wife and two sons. He had managed to conceal his double life for 12 years.

The Mystic Cross: A single, large cross in the Plain of Mars under the Mount of

herself from an emotionally draining relationship when she was 22, it took her a further three years to return to health. Now 44, she has almost forgotten that period, saying that it seems like a bad dream.

A double Line of Life gives added energy and vitality to pursue life's goals, excellent recuperative powers, the ability to remain healthy or to simply remain standing longer when the intake of alcohol is great. These are the people who don't catch the cold or virus that everyone around them is suffering with. Symptoms of ill health usually disappear quickly with those who have a double Line of Life.

A double Line of Head indicates a great mind, and these people can see life from two perspectives at once. They are creative, sensitive, romantic and sentimental, yet analytical, logical and able to complete those things they begin.

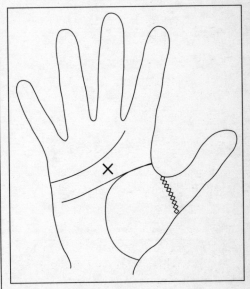

Figure 120 *The Mystic Cross*

Saturn, or between the mounts of Saturn and Apollo, is a sign of strong powers of intuition. It is called the Mystic Cross. If this cross is on the Line of Fate, it can indicate a career in the psychic sciences. If it is on the Line of Sun, the subject could earn a good reputation for psychic or mystical abilities.

Fingernail shapes in a mixed hand: When the subject has a mixed hand (a hand which is a combination of several pure types), I have found that the fingernails follow a pattern:

- the Jupiter finger is slightly more square;
- the Saturn finger is slightly more spatulate; and
- the Apollo finger is often more conic than the others.

Part V
Giving
readings

READING PROCEDURE

Have the subject sit opposite you at a table covered with a white or neutral-coloured cloth. You will require a reading lamp to ensure sufficient light, though I have found that the very best light for palm reading is sunlight. I have heard that in some parts of India palmists read only at sunrise. They believe that the subject's blood circulation and nervous system is likely to be in a more balanced state upon awakening than at any other time of the day. Another reason could be that the sun casts a better angle of light when it cuts across the lines as opposed to bearing directly down upon them. To achieve this effect at any time of the day, simply angle the palms so that the light source cuts across the lines (i.e. at a 90 degree angle). This will increase the shadow effect, making the lines easier to see.

Ask the subject to remove any rings, bracelets or watches. Have the person shake his or her hands vigorously for five seconds to ensure good blood circulation, then place both hands naturally (as they fall) palm downwards on the table.

Relax and take your time.

1. **Note which is the writing hand.**
   If unsure, ask.
2. **Note the size of the hands.**
   The larger the hands, the more the subject prefers detail. The smaller the hands, the more the person prefers large,

even grandiose things, and becomes frustrated with details.

3. **Decide what shape the hands are.**
   Are they both the same shape? If not, keep in mind that the writing hand represents the present and the future whereas the non-writing hand details the past.
4. **Examine the hands.**
   Are there any warts on the hands?
   Is the skin on the back of the hands fine or coarse in texture?
   Is there any hair on the hands? If so, what colour is it?

   When you have examined the back of the hands and detailed your findings, turn them over and begin with a quick check of all the main lines. There is no point discovering a double Line of Head or an absent Line of Heart late into the reading. Now decide whether the palm is firm, soft or hard, and whether it is dry, moist or clammy.
5. **Examine the fingers.**
   Note the length of each finger and whether it is straight. Look for gaps between any fingers (e.g. the little finger sits out on its own).
6. **Note the size, shape and colour of the nails.**
   Are they clear or milky?
   Are they brittle, chewed or smooth?

Do they have any ridges or dips?

Does your subject wear any rings? If so, on which finger/thumb?

Are there noticeable moons in the nails? (Note: the thumbnail moons are always larger than those of the fingers.)

What is the colour under the nails?

Does the colour under the nails match the colour of the palms?

Are the fingers smooth or knotty?

7. **Examine the thumb carefully.**

   Is it straight or flexible at the upper joint?

   Is it set low, medium or high on the hand?

   Is it long or short? Check carefully — a long, low-set thumb can appear to be of average length, and an average length thumb which is set high on the hand can appear to be long.

8. **Determine the primary and secondary mounts.**

   Describe in detail their meanings, and relate this to what you know already (i.e. the shape, colour and texture of the hands).

9. **Describe other important mounts and detail any signs and markings on the primary and secondary mounts.**

10. **Examine the main lines, starting with the Line of Life.**

    Using a felt-tipped pen and a ruler, measure and date the Line of Life and the lines of Fate and Sun. This will help you to date any event you describe to the subject with an accuracy of about 12–18 months. The lines of Fate and Sun will confirm the dates.

Always confirm an event seen on the Line of Life by checking the other main lines. This increases your accuracy in dating events, and the other lines offer more detail about the event.

11. **After you have covered the Line of Life, move on to the Line of Head, then the Line of Heart.**

    You will have already examined these lines to confirm what you saw on the Line of Life, so it will not take very long to cover them again.

12. **Examine the Girdle of Venus if it exists in the subject's hands.**

13. **Now move on to the Line of Fate, then examine the Line of Sun if it is present** (not everyone has a Line of Apollo).

14. **If you have not examined the Family Chain when you examined the lines of Life and Mars, do so now.**

15. **Carefully examine the Line of Health.** This line will often confirm what you have already described through the mounts, and sometimes you will glean further information for the subject.

16. **Examine the Relationship Lines, and then the Lines of Children.**

    Take your time here as these are tiny lines which are easily confused.

17. **Finally, check each phalange of the fingers for lines and signs.**

    When you have completed the reading, ask the subject if he or she has any questions. Once you have answered any questions, conclude the reading on a positive note by repeating some positive observation you have made earlier; for instance, you could say something like 'With your strong Mount of Jupiter and straight Jupiter finger, you have the ability to know an opportunity when you see one. Others may call it luck, but you have good judgement.'

By following the steps above, you will ensure that you do not leave anything out, nor will you forget where you were if you are interrupted. You may prefer a different order of reading, and, if so, that's fine. However, the system I use has the added advantage of ensuring the least number of contradictory statements. It can be frustrating if you find that the perfect relationship you predicted by looking at the Relationship Lines first is cancelled out by the divorce shown by a cross at the end of a sister line to the Line of Life.

You will relate a great deal of information during a full reading, so do not be disheartened if your subject seems a little confused or overwhelmed at the end of the reading. When you feel confident, you may wish to tape your readings, for then your client can make more sense of your reading when listening to it later.

A friend handed me a recording of a reading he had recently received, as it worried him considerably. It began, 'I don't know why you married that girl, for you know it won't last …' and from there it only got worse. My friend had been married only two weeks when he went for this reading. These types of comments are unnecessary and damaging. Constructive criticism is fine, but thinly veiled bitterness is not worth paying for when it can be had for free.

GAINING PRACTICAL EXPERIENCE

I believe that it takes about 25 readings to become familiar with the hand and the basics of palmistry. After 50 readings, you are likely to find that you are flowing more freely, and 100 readings will find you gaining confidence in your ability.

'How am I ever going to find 100 new people to read for in order to gain confidence?' you may well ask. But it is only ten new people a week for ten weeks or five people a week over 20 weeks. Once the word gets around that you're reading palms, people will approach you for a reading.

Reading at markets is how many people gain experience and earn a little pocket money, but you need to be prepared to attend the same market for at least five weeks to allow potential clients to see you at your stall and think about having a reading. Some of my clients admitted to enquiring about a reading six months before actually having one, so be patient.

To ensure a busy day at a market stall, it is wise to read for a friend or to give a free reading to a local stall holder, as I have found that people are more likely to want a reading from a Palmist who is already busy than from someone who is alone, staring into space or reading a book.

Palmistry parties can also provide a worthwhile opportunity to read briefly for 20 or 30 people in one night. I have read at parties in the past and although they can be exhausting, they are usually rewarding.

At one palmistry party, with about 60 or 70 guests, I was hired to read for three hours. I found myself growing tired of telling everyone that they would find psychology appealing, and that investigation would come naturally to them (as indicated by a strong Mount of Pluto). When the thirteenth person in a row thrust her hands under my nose I couldn't bear it any longer.

'Can you tell me how all of these people earn their living? I'm getting tired of saying the same thing to every person I see.'

'Oh, we're all psychiatrists. It's Jackie's birthday and we are her colleagues.'

The next person was the husband of one of the psychiatrists, and I have never been so glad to read for a banker. Aaron was sceptical at first, but my opening comment made him more curious.

'Thank goodness for a pair of hands which show no interest in psychology. It makes a change around here, I can tell you.'

'So what do I do for a living then?' he asked me in a doubtful voice.

'I cannot tell you what you do, but I can tell you what you're suited to. Banking, accountancy and figures generally would suit you.'

Aaron laughed and turned to the woman (another psychiatrist) in the line behind him and said, 'Hey, Marlene, who's been talking to this guy about me?'

As the three hours passed, word travelled about my readings and the hostess appeared with a question.

'How much longer can you stay? There are quite a few people who have just arrived and I have a couple of very special guests who didn't fancy waiting in line.'

I smiled. People love hearing about themselves. I agreed to stay on for an extra hour, as Aaron appeared with a friend and a challenge.

'Paul, this is Bob. I bet you can't pick him as easily as you did me.' Bob eyed me warily and his spatulate hands reminded me to be direct and to the point. With strong mounts of Pluto, Luna and Jupiter, I couldn't help myself.

'You have a great affinity with the water, Bob, but if you went sailing I wonder how you would manage to stay inside the boat. You can be a bit clumsy at times.' Bob's eyes widened and Aaron spilled both the drinks, he was laughing so much.

'We have a joke about Bob when we go sailing. We ask, "Has anyone seen Bob, Bob, Bob?"'

Part VI
Health

HEALTH THROUGH THE HANDS

Health is one of those things we rarely notice until we don't have it any longer. Without good health, few things in life can be fully enjoyed. Our health is immediately apparent in our hands, and health directly or indirectly affects every decision we make in life.

I normally state what I see regarding the subject's health, and advise them to consult a doctor or alternative health practitioner for confirmation or clarification of what I have described. However, unless you are a qualified medical practitioner or alternative health practitioner, do not diagnose, for it is illegal to do so in many countries.

In one reading I gave recently, I listed the health problems likely to be encountered by the client, including allergies to dairy products and several grains, along with neck and throat trouble and a delicate stomach. She consulted a natural therapist soon afterwards, and later told me that 'It was like hearing your reading all over again. She said all that you had said, and more besides.'

The following table details some of the health problems that can be shown by the hand.

HEALTH REFERENCE LIST
A–Z

PROBLEM	WHERE IT SHOWS IN THE HANDS	REFER TO FIGURE
Abdomen	A strong Mount of Pluto, with a cross or grille on the mount.	35
Accidents	A strong Mount of Jupiter, with a grille on the mount.	23
Aneurism	A break in the Line of Heart under the Mount of Saturn, or a strong Mount of Apollo, much lined or grilled.	70
Arms	Accidents to or restrictions with the arms are shown by a strong Mount of Mercury with a large red or black spot.	29
Asthma	Lines of Head and Heart close together, with a much-lined Plain of Mars.	71
Allergies	A full Mount of Luna suggests an allergy to dairy products. Two or three horizontal lines on the first phalange of the Saturn finger (starting from the side of the finger) suggest an allergy to grains. Each line can indicate a particular grain to which the subject might be intolerant (i.e. two lines suggests allergies to two different types of grains).	25 33
Anorexia	A grilled Mount of Venus, often hollow, with a strong Saturn finger and several vertical lines on the mount. It is a combination of a	39

PROBLEM	WHERE IT SHOWS IN THE HANDS	REFER TO FIGURE
	low Mount of Venus (little desire for food or for sensual fulfilment), and strong Saturn finger (a keen sense of deprivation). Added to this there will often be grilled third phalanges of all the fingers, showing a frustration in receiving physical fulfilment.	25
Arthritis	A full Mount of Luna, with a large, in-dependent cross. Instead of a cross there can be a strong, single vertical line.	33
Biliousness	A yellow palm, cold skin and a wavy Line of Health. A much-lined Mount of Saturn or Mercury increases this tendency.	25 29
Bladder or bowel	A full Mount of Pluto, with a cross or grille on the mount or a grille low on the mount.	35
Blindness	Blindness in one eye, or trouble with one eye, is shown by a single circle on the Line of Life. Two circles indicate trouble with both eyes. An island on the Line of Heart under the Mount of Apollo can also indicate eyesight trouble, particularly short- or long-sightedness. (Note: this also is the sign for heart trouble.)	42
Blood loss	An extremely prominent or grilled Mount of Mars.	31
Body odour	A full Mount of Luna, strong Mount of Saturn (a disinclination to wash regularly) and soft hands. These signs indicate a slow lymphatic system, which leaves the subject's body choked up with waste. This waste (or some of it) finds its way out of the body	25 33

	through the skin, producing the odour. These people tend to have blocked nasal passages, and so are unable to smell their own odour.	
Bulimia	A strong, full Mount of Venus, often much lined or grilled, grilled third phalanges of the fingers, a strong or much-lined Mount of Saturn and a Girdle of Venus. The full Mount of Venus shows a love of food and eating, while the strong Mount of Saturn encourages deprivation and increases guilt. The grilled third phalanges of the fingers show frustration at receiving physical pleasure and fulfilment. The grilled Mount of Venus often shows someone who eats rapidly, as though starving. If a strong Girdle of Venus is present, check for lines of influence running to the Mount of Saturn from inside the Line of Life, and encourage the person to resolve the issues which occurred at the ages where the Lines of Influence cross the Line of Life.	25 39 78
Cancer	As cancer can affect almost any part of the body, it is more likely to show as difficulties in a particular part of the body, than as cancer. I have yet to research cancer wards and hospices to gather any conclusive evidence of how cancer shows in the hands.	
Chest & lungs	A strong, much-lined Mount of Mercury and close Lines of Head and Heart or long, narrow nails, show a tendency towards problems with the chest and lungs.	29 62
Colds	A full, much-lined Mount of Luna and no Line of Mars, or hollow or flat mounts of	33

PROBLEM	WHERE IT SHOWS IN THE HANDS	REFER TO FIGURE
	Upper and Lower Mars, or a much-lined Mount of Luna and soft, flabby hands.	
Constipation	Strong mounts of Luna and Pluto, and nails which curve inwards (hooked nails). Also, the fingers tend to curl up when relaxed.	33 35
Deafness	Dots on the Line of Head under the Mount of Saturn, and sometimes an island, plus a strong, much-lined Mount of Saturn and a much-lined or grilled Mount of Mercury. (Saturn represents restrictions, Mercury represents communication.)	25 29
Diabetes & hypoglycaemia	Cross lines on the lower part of the Mount of Luna or on the Mount of Pluto, or three or more tiny vertical lines above but touching the Line of Heart between Mercury and Apollo.	80
Digestive problems	A Line of Health consisting of many short lines from the Mount of Mercury to the Line of Life, or a grilled Mount of Venus, and sometimes strong Mounts of Luna and Upper Mars. The Mount of Upper Mars indicates a love of hot, spicy foods, while a sensitive stomach is shown by the strong Mount of Luna.	30 32 39 104
Dizziness	The Line of Head terminating on or above the Line of Heart on the Mount of Mercury.	
Eyes	see Blindness	
Exhaustion	A soft hand without elasticity; a palm and fingers which feel half filled with sand.	28

PROBLEM	WHERE IT SHOWS IN THE HANDS	REFER TO FIGURE
	When you press the mounts or fingers they do not bounce back. With a strong Mount of Mercury, it may be nervous exhaustion and with a strong Mount of Lower Mars, it could be adrenal exhaustion.	
Feet (cold)	Blue-tinged, moonless nails and a strong Mount of Neptune.	37
Fevers	Red dots on the Line of Life suggest fevers, and these dots can sometimes be found on the Line of Head. Often a broken Line of Health accompanies these dots.	
Gall badder	Yellowish hands and a strong Mount of Saturn, much-lined or grilled.	25
Gout	A much-lined or grilled Mount of Jupiter.	23
Glandular imbalance	An overweight person with very puffy third phalanges on the back of the fingers, and flat third phalanges on the front, has a possible thyroid problem.	
Headaches	A strong Mount of Lower Mars or a strong Line of Mars.	97
Hips	A grille on the Mount of Jupiter and a crooked Jupiter finger.	23
Heart trouble	A chained, badly broken Line of Heart or an absent Line of Heart; a large island on the Line of Heart under the Mount of Apollo; a grilled Mount of Apollo; bulbous tips to the fingers and thumbs, with an almost swollen appearance; or a series of large dots on the	27 70 73

Line of Heart. Blue-tinged nails indicate a poor heart and, in turn, poor blood circulation. A break in the Line of Heart under the Mount of Mercury denotes liver trouble affecting the heart.

PROBLEM	WHERE IT SHOWS IN THE HANDS	REFER TO FIGURE
Haemorrhoids	A much-lined Mount of Saturn and strong mounts of Luna and Pluto.	25 33 35
Hypochondria	Five vertical lines on the Mount of Mercury (medical stigmata), with a Line of Head that curves into a very full Mount of Luna (fears). Luna intensifies the preoccupation with self.	28 65
Indigestion	A wavy Line of Health, an island on the Line of Life and a weak or broken up Line of Head; or strong vertical ridges in all the fingernails.	12 103
Injuries to the head	A strong Mount of Lower Mars, or dots on the Line of Head, or a long Line of Mars.	31
Insanity (temporary)	A clearly defined island on the Line of Head can suggest a nervous breakdown or a period of great mental confusion. If the line returns to normal afterwards, all is eventually well with the subject's mental health.	
Insanity (in old age, senility)	The Line of Head weakens or breaks into a series of tiny lines after crossing the Line of Health. If this is evident in both hands, it could be hereditary. A star on the Line of Head on the Mount of Luna also indicates senility.	33
Jaundice	Yellow hands and strong lines or a grille on the mounts of Saturn or Mercury.	25 29

PROBLEM	WHERE IT SHOWS IN THE HANDS	REFER TO FIGURE
Joints	A full Mount of Luna with a large cross or a single vertical line in the centre of the mount. (These are similar signs to those indicating arthritis.)	33
Kidney trouble	Many lines on the lower part of Luna, a cross on the lower part of Luna, or a long line, starting from the edge of the hand on the Mount of Luna and terminating in a fork, just before reaching the Line of Life.	33
Knees	A strong Mount of Saturn, much-lined or grilled.	25
Legs	Accidents to the shins show with dots or crosses on the Mount of Saturn. Accidents to the thighs are indicated by dots on the Mount of Jupiter.	25 33
Liver	Cold, damp skin, yellow hands and a much-lined Mount of Mercury. The main lines will be yellow. The Line of Health may be yellowish and formed in a ladder-like series of tiny lines. Dark spots on the Mount of Luna can also indicate liver trouble.	29 33 104
Lymphatic system slow	A strong Mount of Luna and soft, flabby hands.	33
Lung	see Asthma; Chest & lungs	
Memory loss	A dot, followed by a break in the Line of Head, indicates memory loss from an accident to the head. If the memory loss is due to senility or old age, it shows as a weakening Line of Head or a Line of Head breaking into tiny lines after crossing the Line of Health.	

PROBLEM	WHERE IT SHOWS IN THE HANDS	REFER TO FIGURE
Moodiness	A Girdle of Venus, a strong double or triple Girdle of Venus, or a full Mount of Luna with a deeply sloping Line of Head indicates extreme sensitivity to criticism and a sulky nature.	33 37 79
Mood swings (highs and lows in quick succession)	A Girdle of Venus, plus four or five tiny vertical lines just above or touching the Line of Heart between the mounts of Apollo and Mercury, suggests blood sugar fluctuations which could be due to problems with the pancreas.	78 80
Menstrual problems	Much-lined or grilled mounts of Luna or Pluto. Several tiny crosses on the Mount of Pluto can relate to problems with the female reproductive organs, and with a larger cross on a full Mount of Pluto, this could require a hysterectomy or alternative medical treatment at some stage in the subject's life. Without these signs, but with a strong Girdle of Venus, look for emotional causes.	33 35 78
Nose bleeds	Regular nose bleeds are shown by excessive lower and upper Mounts of Mars, often with a grille on the upper mount.	31
Nervous system	Problems with the central nervous system are indicated by nails which bend upwards and away from the fingers at the point where they leave the fingertips. These people often get 'the shakes' when tired or run down, and if you ask them to hold their hands 30 centimetres above the table, you will notice a slight tremor in the fingers. Often the main lines are a series of chains. A full Mount of	29

PROBLEM	WHERE IT SHOWS IN THE HANDS	REFER TO FIGURE
	Mercury contributes to a nervous disposition.	
Neck/throat	A low-set Mount of Venus with a 'musician's thumb' and four or five tiny vertical lines on the upper Mount of Mars. A low-set Mount of Venus indicates tension in the neck and shoulders, and the vertical lines on the upper Mount of Mars relate to suppressing feelings; losing your temper but saying nothing, for instance.	7 31
Pancreas; _see also Diabetes_	Three or more tiny vertical lines just above or touchingthe Line of Heart between the Mounts Mercury and Apollo.	80
Paralysis	A much-lined Mount of Saturn or a star on the Mount of Saturn. Often a grille or a star on the Mount of Luna. The Line of Life will show a date where a branch from the Line of Health crosses it. The Line of Life will weaken after the Line of Health crosses or touches it.	25 33 102
Poison	The act of being poisoned shows as a large dot on the Line of Head under the Mount of Saturn. Mild poisoning of the body through poor diet, or drugs and alcohol, or through allergies, shows as a line which begins at the percussion and extends across the Mount of Pluto. If this line reaches the Line of Life, the condition is serious.	25 35
Reproductive _organs_	Any dots, crosses or grilles on the Mount of Pluto indicate difficulties with the reproductive organs for both men and women.	35

PROBLEM	WHERE IT SHOWS IN THE HANDS	REFER TO FIGURE
Rheumatism	Strongly lined mounts of Saturn or Luna, or a large cross on the Mount of Luna, or a large, single, vertical line down the centre of the mount. Blue or red dots on the Line of Heart indicate severe bouts of rheumatism if found with the above signs.	25 33
Shins/ankles	A long, full, spatulate-tipped Apollo finger, with a full Mount of Apollo or a Line of Sun strengthening the mount.	
Skin allergies	A strong, lined, Mount of Saturn, and sometimes a dry palm with a yellow tinge to it. Check the nails and the skin colour under the nails. If the skin under the nails is pink or red, the skin condition is temporary. If it is yellow, this is a long-term condition.	25
Shoulder tension	A low-set Mount of Venus.	
Spine	The Mount of Saturn rules the bones generally, so a much-lined or grilled Mount of Saturn, plus a grille on the Mount of Mercury, and stiff fingers and thumbs, shows an inflexibility of bones and spine. The apex of the Mount of Apollo centred close to the Mount of Saturn confirms this.	25 29
Stomach	A delicate stomach is indicated by a full Mount of Luna, and crosses or additional lines on the mount. A Line of Health which is long but ladder-like in its formation confirms digestive and stomach problems.	33 100 104
Teeth	Teeth which decay prematurely are shown by a strong Mount of Saturn, and vertical	25 103

PROBLEM	WHERE IT SHOWS IN THE HANDS	REFER TO FIGURE
	lines or a grille only strengthen the tendencies. The apex of the mount is centred close to the base, of the finger. A long and wavy Line of Health and long second phalanges on all the fingers also appear.	
Toes	*see Feet*	
Throat	Four or five vertical lines on the Mount of Upper Mars and horizontal lines reaching across the Mount of Mars from the percussion. A low-set but full Mount of Venus contributes to the tendency for throat and neck problems.	31
Ulcers (stomach)	A strong, much-lined Mount of Luna and a drooping Line of Head indicate a tendency to worry unduly. Low mounts of Venus, Jupiter, Apollo and Mars show someone who lacks the vitality to do something to resolve his or her worries. Internalised, these concerns can cause ulcers.	33
Varicose veins	A grilled Mount of Jupiter, sometimes with a bent Jupiter finger. The apex of the Mount of Jupiter will be close to the Mount of Saturn.	23
Warts	*see page 30*	
Weight — *overweight*	A strong Mount of Jupiter and a full Mount of Venus show a love of food and plenty of it. Regardless of their physical build, these people can eat 'like a horse'. With a full Mount of Luna, soft, flabby hands, and average mounts of Jupiter and Venus, the	23 32 39

PROBLEM	WHERE IT SHOWS IN THE HANDS	REFER TO FIGURE
	weight is usually the result of liquid retained in the body due to a slow lymphatic system and a disdain for physical exercise. These people drink a great deal of coffee, tea, water or soft drinks to refresh the mouth, and this liquid often stays in their body for longer than it would in other types.	
	Jupiterians hold their weight in the buttocks, hips and thighs. In later years, thetop and bottom halves of the body can appear to be mismatched. The bottom half of the Jupiterian's body will often retain its firmness with increased weight, as these people enjoy exercise.	
	When the mounts of Jupiter and Venus are only average, and the third phalanges of the fingers are thin on the front of the hands (palm side) but full and puffy on the back, excess weight could be due to a glandular imbalance. A check with a qualified medical or alternative practitioner is warranted.	
Weight *— underweight*	A strong Mount of Saturn with poor mounts of Venus and Jupiter. A Girdle of Venus contributes to poor absorption of nutrients from food. A full Mount of Mercury speeds up the metabolism, encouraging the person to live on nervous energy.	24 28 78

GLOSSARY

Fluted nails: Fingernails which bend away from the fingertips once the nail leaves the finger. The longer the nail, the more noticeable the upturn of the nail.

Knotty fingers: Fingers with prominent knuckles.

Percussion: The edge of the palm stretching from the base of the Mercury (little) finger to the wrist.

Phalange: From the word *phalanx*, referring to any of the bones in the fingers. A phalange is one segment of the finger, containing one bone.

Rascette: The lines which cross the wrist at the base of the hand. If the uppermost bracelet is strong and clear, it can confirm a strong physical constitution. Also known as *bracelets*.

Ridged nails: Ridged or grooved nails usually have a series of grooves from the tip to the base of the nail, Sometimes sideways ridging can occur, but this usually grows out within six months.

Smooth fingers: Fingers which are smooth from tip to base, with no broadening around the joints.

BIBLIOGRAPHY

Benham, William G. 1983, *Laws Of Scientific Hand Reading*, D.B. Taraporevala Sons & Co. by arrangement with Putnam & Co., London, UK.

Chambers, Howard V. 1966, *An Occult Dictionary for the Millions*, Sherbourne Press, Los Angeles, USA.

Cheiro, Count Louis Hamon 1977, *You and Your Hand*, Sphere Books, London, UK.

—— 1975, *Cheiro's Language of the Hand*, Corgi Books, London, UK.

—— 1969, *Confessions: Memoirs of a Modern Seer*, Sagar Publications, New Delhi, India.

Gibran, Kahlil 1964, *The Prophet*, William Heinemann, London, UK.

Hope, Murray 1985, *The Way of Cartouche*, Angus & Robertson, Sydney, Australia.

Lofthus, Myrna 1983, *A Spiritual Approach to Astrology*, CRCS Publications, Los Angeles, USA.

Saint-Germain, Comte C. de 1980, *The Study of Palmistry*, Coles Publishing Co., Toronto, Canada.

Index